THE BOOK OF
WOODEN BOATS

VOLUME II

THE BOOK OF
WOODEN BOATS

VOLUME II

Photographs by Benjamin Mendlowitz

Text by Maynard Bray

W. W. NORTON & COMPANY

NEW YORK • LONDON

For Deborah and Anne

Other books of photography by Benjamin Mendlowitz:
Wood, Water & Light
A Passage in Time
The Book of Wooden Boats
The Guide to Wooden Boats
The Guide to Wooden Power Boats

Text copyright © 2001 by Maynard Bray
Photographs copyright © 2001 by Benjamin Mendlowitz
All rights reserved.

The text of this book is composed in Goudy
Book design by Sherry Streeter, Brooklin, Maine
Production by NOAH Publications, Brooklin, Maine
Printed by Dai Nippon Printing Co., Hong Kong

First Edition

Library of Congress Cataloging-in-Publication Data

Mendlowitz, Benjamin
    The book of wooden boats / photographs by Benjamin Mendlowitz:
text by Maynard Bray.
        p.   cm.
    Includes index.
    ISBN 0-393-03417-8
    1. Wooden boats.   2. Wooden boats—United States.   3. Ships.
Wooden.   4. Ships, Wooden—United States.   I. Bray, Maynard.

II. Title
VM321.M45   1992
623.8'207—dc20

ISBN 0-393-04899-3

W.W. Norton & Company, Inc., 500 Fifth Avenue, New York, N.Y. 10110
W.W. Norton & Company, Ltd., 10 Coptic Street, London WC1A 1PU

1 2 3 4 5 6 7 8 9 0

CONTENTS

III. WORKING BOATS

IV. OPEN BOATS

V. SAILING YACHTS

FOREWORD

At first blush, there appears to be something magical about a photograph by Benjamin Mendlowitz. To the casual observer, it might be simply the choice of subject: classic wooden boats, under sail, power, oar, or paddle—or at rest—photographed in some of the world's most beautiful locations. A skeptic might say it would be hard to not take a good photograph of such a subject; it would merely take a trained photographer with a beautiful boat before him, and a high-power zoom lens to allow a close up view, or a wide-angle one to add distance when there is none. A dark boatshed, like the one sheltering the International One-Designs on page 50, might be brought to the proper lighting conditions with strobe lights, reflective boards, power packs, and a web of extension cords hidden from the scene—like a little movie set. And, if all else fails, an almost-perfect image could be loaded into a computer and made right with a few keystrokes.

The skeptic would be wrong. He might also be surprised to learn that the photographer, Benjamin Mendlowitz, does not use a truckload of equipment; he carries all of his essential gear in a shoulder bag—his process echoing the simple harmony of his subject boats. In short, if magic is supernatural illusion, if it requires gadgetry and slight of hand, then there's none here. There are no shape-distorting high-powered lenses, no electric lights or eventual concessions to digital manipulation; and, there's very little pure luck.

The images are carefully planned, and are an honest representation of what the human eye sees. The lighting is done by sun alone. When the film is developed, the scene is complete—standing as a testament to a real moment, never to be changed.

A study of the making of an image by Benjamin Mendlowitz and a knowledge of his professional values reveal something pure—something profound in its economy. The process begins with the carefully chosen subjects, the boats, which are hand-selected for both their beauty and their singularity. All are viewed from a perfect angle, and the backgrounds complement the subjects just so. Consider Benjamin Mendlowitz at work: watch him eyeing a bank of clouds moving into his field of view, or a sliver of clear sky on the horizon, an hour before sunset, and see him gently, persistently suggest to the crew that they scrub this stain, coil that line, drop that dodger, stow that flag, change that shirt—all the while, the shutter has not opened once. And then, as if it were choreographed, the sun explodes from under the clouds and the boat passes before a spruce-clad granite outcropping—hours of preparation for a few select minutes of film exposure.

This is not to say that Benjamin Mendlowitz stages his scenes, because he does not. Rather, it's to say that he has a unique understanding of the shapes of boats and how they blend with the natural world. He has a profound respect for the delicate interplay of natural light, shadow, and color, and for the vintage quality of wooden boats. He does not attempt to override any of this with artificial elements; he instead arranges the natural elements in his photographs to synergistic effect, or anticipates the pieces coming together, and then uses them to a masterful end.

Speaking of synergism, Maynard Bray has for years collaborated with Benjamin Mendlowitz. Maynard, a watercraft historian, boatbuilder, and writer, is responsible for the fine captions that accompany the photographs in Benjamin's *Calendar of Wooden Boats* and, including this one, four of his books. Just as Benjamin photographs with a minimum of equipment, so Maynard writes by filtering his encyclopedic knowledge through a few carefully chosen words. He brings to his writing a lifelong passion for wooden boats: a childhood in boatyards in Rockland, Maine; stints building ships at Connecticut's Electric Boat and Maine's Bath Iron Works; years of research and hands-on work at Mystic Seaport Museum supervising the rebuilding of the watercraft collection there; a lifelong fascination with, and study of, the Herreshoff Manufacturing Company; and numerous reconstructions of historic boats accomplished under his guidance. His knowledge is far more than a simple list of facts; he has a unique depth of understanding of wooden boats both large and small.

The Book of Wooden Boats, volumes I and II, serve as a collection of images and captions that first appeared in the *Calendar of Wooden Boats*. Over the past 18 years, the Calendar has grown into a tradition in itself for wooden boat enthusiasts everywhere. Like the twelve images in it, the simple elegance of the Calendar belies the major effort that goes into its production each year—the numerous research and photography trips, the tracking down of boat owners, the logistics of the photo shoot, the researching and writing of the captions—and the selection of twelve images from among thousands.

Benjamin Mendlowitz's photography books—*Wood, Water & Light, A Passage in Time, The Book of Wooden Boats, The Guide to Wooden Boats,* and *The Guide to Wooden Power Boats*—give us a glimpse of the quality and sheer number of photographs that are considered for the Calendar each year. These images and the words that accompany them provide a breath of fresh air in a world hard-fallen for gadgetry and disposability.

A single picture in the Calendar graces our offices, homes, and lives for just a month at a time. Fortunately, we have this book to preserve those images and draw from Benjamin Mendlowitz's rich portfolio to show us added details of the boats we've come to treasure; it's a book we'll return to often through the years. That one month is never enough.

Matthew P. Murphy
Editor, *WoodenBoat* magazine

INTRODUCTION

Nearly a decade has passed since Volume I of *The Book of Wooden Boats* was published. At that time, it appeared that wooden boats were rapidly vanishing with few, if any, new ones replacing them. In that book's introduction, I referred to wooden boats as "a valuable heritage in peril." Well, I'm happy to report that things are changing for the better. Wooden boatbuilding and restoration are enjoying a renaissance, in both this country and Europe, as this book goes to press. A booming economy seems to have teamed up with a growing desire for the classic beauty and traditional craftsmanship found in yachts and boats individually built of wood. Fortunately, there are enough skilled boatbuilders to fulfill the demand—but only just enough! Boatshops are humming with activity and are turning out some exceptional work. Some of the recently completed projects are shown in the following pages. *Curlew, Elizabeth Muir, Grace, Madigan, Mimi Rose, Vela, White Wings*, and *Wild Horses* are powerful examples of new construction carried out over the past decade. Major restorations during that time are represented by *Grayling, Principia, Quill II, Teaser, Thendara*, and *Tuiga*. It appears that we'll not be running out of fine wooden boats to photograph anytime soon, nor will boatbuilders be running out of worthwhile projects in the near future.

You'll find within these pages many boats that were photographed near where we live in Maine. To be sure, it's more convenient near home, and we can't help but be drawn to all the great wooden boats on this part of the coast. It's become a wooden boat Mecca, a homeport for many and summertime cruising ground for more. Other parts of the country, such as California and the Pacific Northwest, also have good boats and you'll find a sampling of those too. Outstanding boats from all along the US East Coast, the Caribbean, and Europe have been chased down and photographed as well. In this book, we have supplemented each original calendar image with one or two additional views so you can more fully appreciate how beautiful these boats really are. The dimensions given for each boat represent the overall length and maximum beam of the hull proper.

Although digital cameras are constantly improving, slow speed, fine grain 35mm slide film is still Benjamin's choice for capturing the ultimate image out on the water. And although it is now easy to manipulate these images through digitization, adding or eliminating various features, that has never happened to any of the photos in *The Calendar of Wooden Boats* or within this book. The images you see here are exactly as the camera saw them when the shutter was clicked. But there's considerable fussing in getting a boat to look as good as it possibly can before we begin shooting. Lots of film is used in getting the best picture that measures up in all respects, and great care is taken in reproducing the slide on the printed page. We think the results are worth the effort, and hope that you agree.

Maynard Bray
Brooklin, Maine

ACKNOWLEDGMENTS

The name on a transom tells us a lot about the feeling an owner has for his boat. I have always been amused by the quirky names I stumble across as I explore a harbor, passing countless modern boats while seeking out the one or two classic gems that might be lying somewhere hidden from view. Just last week in Hope Town I found my all-time favorite on a homely, run-down cruising cutter named *Sailbad the Sinner*, finally surpassing the candidate-sinking sport fisherman, *Monkey Business*. As I continued my harbor tour laughing to myself at the clever word play, I briefly thought of renaming *Starlight*. The idea vanished moments later for the simple reason that I have too much respect for her to give her a wacky name, no matter how amusing it would be.

As I look through the boats in this book and study the care and devotion given to them by their designers, builders and owners, I realize that all must share this basic respect, if not a deep love and appreciation, of what they have created and possess in these fine craft. The names they give tell the story. Many are named after women. Although we know they were all cherished, we're left to wonder if they were mothers, daughters, wives or lovers: *Hannah, Edna Kathleen, Charlena, Grace, Roann, Miss Robin, Alice, Anne Marie, Elizabeth Muir, Clio, Abigail, Jessica, Mariella.* The male names seem given out of love and respect for a relative or mentor: *Walter & Edgar, Gramp, Jacob Pike, Spike Africa, Breck Marshall, Nathaniel Bowditch, Lewis R. French.* There are names of people's favorite things: *Clover, Morning Star, Quiet Tune, Albacore, Owl, Meadows, Harmony, Buttercup,* even an opera, *Aida.* Owners with speed or racing on their minds give names like: *Wild Horses, White Wings, Triple Threat, Typhoon, Banzai, Teaser.* Some of the boats go right to the heart of the matter and carry names evoking grandeur, adventure and pride: *Endeavour, Alert, Californian, Pride of Baltimore, Heritage, Unity B, Principia, Mohican, Courageous, Pacifica, Brigadoon, Ticonderoga, Escapade, Dauntless, Voyager.* A play on words leans towards poetry not farce in *Tranquil C.*

All these names so carefully painted on, some even gilded, show respect for the boats and the people who design, build and care for them. This book, like the first volume, is made possible by those same people, and the wonderful boats that they have created and maintained. We thank you all for your efforts and devotion and hope that this volume does justice to your pride and joy. The design and production of this book takes care and effort as well and Maynard and I would like to acknowledge those who have contributed so much to this endeavor: Julie Mattes for her tireless typesetting, editing and attention to details large and small. Anita Jacobssen for her management of the photo collection and her help with the photo selection. Sherry Streeter for her elegant design work. Matt Murphy, the editor at *WoodenBoat* magazine, for his generous thoughts in the foreword. Jim Mairs, our editor at W.W. Norton, for his continuous support and interest in this work and commitment to quality. Our wives Anne Bray and Deborah Brewster who have helped with the editing and who are such an integral part of our lives, on and off the water, at home and at this, our work.

Benjamin Mendlowitz
Brooklin, Maine

THE BOOK OF
WOODEN BOATS

VOLUME II

CHAPTER I

SAILBOATS

Sailing offers a chance to move towards your destination without the smell, noise, or expense of an engine. Motion through the water will be steadied by the pressure of the wind on the rig, so these boats roll much less than a similarly sized powerboat. This chapter features some of the finest sailboats ever built. They can be handled by one or two people, cared for by the owner if he or she chooses, and yet are roomy enough for cruising in comfort. They make great family boats where children learn sailing technique, coastal navigation, and how to care for what might become a family heirloom. Given reasonable but consistent maintenance, boats like this can serve several generations, and it makes little difference how old a boat is when it comes to having a good time. *Freda* is an inspiring example.

   Freda passed her centennial in 1985 and, not surprisingly, has become somewhat of a legend in her home waters of San Francisco Bay. But sailors far beyond have heard of her, and those privileged to have seen her have come away filled with admiration. *Freda* is a native of the Bay—her Sausalito slip is within sight of where she was built in 1885—but she looks out on a scene greatly changed from those post-Gold Rush days. There were no internal-combustion engines, no skyscrapers lined the horizon, and bridging the Golden Gate was but a dream. So common was working sail back then that *Freda* would scarcely have been noticed. Now, however, she's a unique survivor.

FREDA, *a gaff sloop*   *LOA: 33'0"*   *Beam: 12'2"*   *Modeled and built 1885 by*
Harry Cookson, Belvedere, California   Photographed on San Francisco Bay, California

ACADIA

A Friendship sloop

You can understand why Friendship sloops have remained popular: They're among the handsomest of all the traditional workboats. A hundred years ago, they were the favored lobsterboats of mid-coast Maine; 60 years ago, after engines caught on, aging Friendships made economical pleasureboat conversions; and 40 years ago, the Friendship Sloop Society came into being and ensured that Friendships would never be forgotten. New Friendships began appearing, with 12 of the wooden ones coming from Ralph Stanley's shop, including *Acadia*. While not exactly a single-hander with all five sails set, a Friendship sloop's rig can be shortened down to suit about any crew size or weather. In the days of commercial sail, a lobsterman would set only the mainsail and jumbo—his name for the boomed forestaysail. By playing one sheet against the other, he could remain dead in the water while bringing a trap aboard, and then by sheeting in the jumbo, spin away and head for the next pot buoy.

LOA: 28'0"   Beam: 10'0"
Designed and built 1998 by Ralph W. Stanley,
  Southwest Harbor, Maine
Photographed in Somes Sound, Maine

QUILL II

A cruising yawl

Quill II is a boat of multiple distinctions. John F. Cole had her designed and built in 1905 and owned her for the next 57 years, sailing and cruising all that time without an engine. She is the oldest extant boat from the prolific Hodgdon Bros. shop. Her sail plan and lines were drawn by 21-year-old John G. Alden while he worked in the office of B.B. Crowninshield and before he embarked upon his own world-famous yacht-design business. Most recently, after a 30-year absence, this gaff yawl—nearly all original—has returned to a mooring not 10 miles distant from Bucks Harbor where Cole kept her all those years.

    Quill II's freeboard is low by today's standards, so it doesn't take much of a wave to splash water aboard. But compared to his first *Quill*, a racy knockabout, *Quill II* was, for John Cole, a craft of eminent wholesomeness.

LOA: 38'0"   Beam: 9'10"
Designed by B.B. Crowninshield
Built 1905 by Hodgdon Bros., East Boothbay, Maine
Photographed on Eggemoggin Reach, Maine

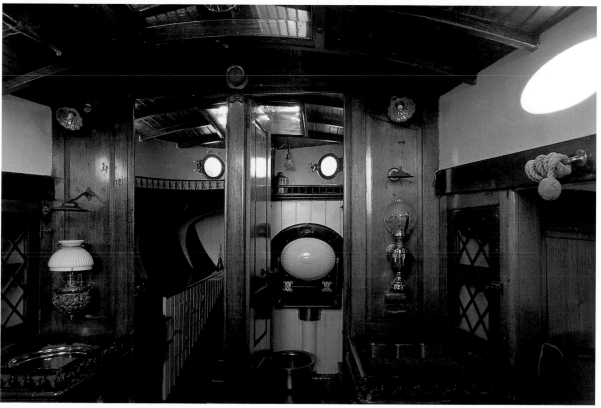

CONJURER

A Cape Cod catboat

The Crosby catboat *Conjurer* comes from another era—an era when auxiliary power was rare in cruising sailboats, when you used big sails rather than engines to keep going in light air. *Conjurer* now has a marine engine, but if you decide not to spoil a beautiful evening like this by using it, you'll be just as glad as the old-timers were to have that 550-square-foot mainsail. You'll ghost back to the mooring thankful for the ample spread of canvas. For a brisk afternoon sou'wester, however, you'll soon learn that the sail is too big for the breeze and that *Conjurer* will move faster and steer better with that big sail reefed.

LOA: 27'0"   Beam: 12'0"
Modeled and built 1909 by H. Manley Crosby,
*   Osterville, Massachusetts*
Photographed on Eggemoggin Reach, Maine

BRECK MARSHALL

A Cape Cod catboat

It isn't always easy for interested people to find a good traditional boat to try out. Recognizing this, Mystic Seaport Museum several years ago established a boat livery featuring dories, pulling boats, skiffs, some small sailboats, and the museum-built Cape Cod catboat *Breck Marshall*. After demonstrating reasonable proficiency, you can rent any of these good wooden boats by the hour and test their performance. But proficient or not, anyone can sign up for a half-hour sail in the *Breck Marshall*, as one of the six passengers she can legally carry, and watch some exceptionally fine boat handling. Although sailing in light winds can be tricky on a busy river with a noticeable current, the skipper is so in tune with the boat and the situation that he makes these trips appear completely relaxed. At $4 per person, this is a bargain as well as an education, so it's little wonder that some 5,000 people sign up each year for a sail aboard the *Breck Marshall*.

LOA: 20'0"   Beam: 9'8"
Designed by Charles Crosby
Built 1987 by Brent Laurent, Clark Poston, and
*   Barry Thomas of Mystic Seaport Museum,*
*   Mystic, Connecticut*
Photographed on the Mystic River, Connecticut

BANZAI

A New York 30 class sloop

A shout of joy like Hurrah! At least 10,000 years and maybe forever. These are a couple of the most appropriate translations for this yacht's name—a yacht built more than 90 years ago that can still bring joy to the helmsperson, crew, and onlookers. *Banzai* is number 15 of the 18-boat fleet of New York 30 class gaff-rigged sloops launched in April of 1905 from the shops of the Herreshoff Mfg. Co. In all those years, *Banzai*'s name was considered good enough to leave unchanged, and in all that time—despite two world wars, a major economic depression, and vastly changing social customs—these boats were well-enough built and so highly regarded for their looks and performance that more than half of them are still sailing. To that we shout, "Banzai!"

LOA: 43'6"   Beam: 8'10"
Designed by N.G. Herreshoff
Built 1905 by Herreshoff Mfg. Co., Bristol,
    Rhode Island
Photographed at Vineyard Haven, Massachusetts

BUZZARDS BAY 25

A keel/centerboard sloop

Building a plank-on-frame hull upside down eases the task of planking because the work is below you and there's better light than with the hull upright. Nathanael Herreshoff pioneered the method as well as the practice of bending frames directly over temporary molds. Here, the boat's yellow pine backbone—the stem and keel—has been lowered into place over the frame assemblies and planking is about to begin. When completed, this yet-unnamed boat will sail out of Marion, Massachusetts, where the original boats, then known as Herreshoff Specials, first raced from the Beverly Yacht Club in 1915. That fleet—never more than five boats strong—has long been scattered, although four still exist. The design, nowadays called a Buzzards Bay 25, has enjoyed a renaissance in recent years in new construction, both conventional planking and cold-molding. It's easy to see why: Even before planking commences, the graceful proportions of this exceptional design clearly show. And completed boats, like the cold-molded *High Cotton*, take your breath away.

LOA: 33′2″   Beam: 8′9″
Designed by N.G. Herreshoff
Under construction 1996 by Ballentine's Boat Shop,
    Cataumet, Massachusetts

HIGH COTTON (above right)
LOA: 32′0″   Beam: 8′9″
Designed by N.G. Herreshoff
Built 1995 by Brooklin Boat Yard, Brooklin, Maine
Photographed in Center Harbor, Maine

AIDA

A keel/centerboard cruising yawl

She'll float in only about three feet of water, so this yawl's cruising grounds extend acres beyond the average 34-footer's. Yet, because of a goodly chunk of outside, cast-lead ballast, *Aida* can carry a normal sail plan which, in turn, means that she's no slouch in light air. Inside the cabin, scant head-room—only about 5'6"—is the price you pay for the shallow draft and lovely above-water profile. For over 30 years, I've been only too glad to stoop a little in the cabin of this wonderful boat of ours, and neither Anne nor I would change a single thing about her layout, especially her big, comfortable cockpit and forward-placed galley. *Aida* is a one-of-a-kind from the Herreshoffs of Bristol, Rhode Island, a version of Capt. Nat's own yawl *Pleasure*, slightly enlarged for coastal cruising. (*Pleasure*, now at the Herreshoff Marine Museum, was intended more as a day boat.) How fine it would be if other variations of this basic design found in Herreshoff proposal drawings were someday built.

LOA: 33'6"   Beam: 9'2"
Designed by N.G. Herreshoff
Built 1926 by Herreshoff Mfg. Co., Bristol,
*   Rhode Island*
Photographed on Eggemoggin Reach, Maine

TEASER

A Newport 29 class sloop

They say that even if little of the original boat remains after restoration, the craft still retains its original soul—provided that the replacement took place piece by piece and that one could always recognize an entity called a boat. By that rationale—actually quite a good one—*Teaser* will come out of this operation with her soul intact. Restoring an aging Herreshoff sailboat like this 1926 Newport 29 class sloop can be very gratifying. Her builder used brass and bronze fastenings almost everywhere so little if any deterioration came from rusting steel or iron. Sometimes the original pieces can be reused, or at least be salvaged enough to serve as patterns for new ones. Is going at it like this more work than building new? Perhaps, but those owners find more than enough extra value in the soul they helped save.

LOA: 36′9″   Beam: 10′6″
Designed by N.G. Herreshoff
Built 1926 by Herreshoff Mfg. Co., Bristol,
    Rhode Island
Photographed at Ballentine's Boat Shop, Cataumet,
    Massachusetts

ALBACORE

A cruising ketch

Sixty years ago, getting a boat out of the water almost always took place on a railway like the one *Albacore* sits on here. Designers of *Albacore*'s era kept hauling needs in mind and, more often than not, specified a straight length of keel for the purpose of landing securely on the rail car or cradle. *Albacore* not only fits a railway but fits in with the rest of what we see here—because wood has been the material of choice for most of the buildings as well as the boats at Benjamin River Marine. *Albacore* is a lucky boat. She has always attracted good owners who have kept her well—and with her pedigree, why wouldn't she? Not only is her design a joy to behold, but the quality of her construction is superb. She's here for a complete restoration, and when launching time comes, instead of Cuttyhunk, she'll carry her new hailing port—Brooklin—on her transom. The name *Albacore* will remain, however; it's never been otherwise!

LOA: 40'8"   Beam: 12'0"
Designed by L. Francis Herreshoff
*Built 1929 by George F. Lawley & Son, Neponset,
     Massachusetts*
Photographed in mid-coast Maine

MINARET

An Araminta ketch

In creating a boat today, beauty often takes a back seat to other considerations, such as initial cost, utility, and performance. Cookie-cutter "product boats" are the natural outcome of such priorities, but as a boat ages, it's her visual appeal that determines whether or not she'll be considered a cherished classic. Fortunately, with his design number 89, L. Francis Herreshoff had a client, Edwin Hill, who encouraged him to draw a thing of beauty. The result was the ketch *Araminta*, built by Norman Hodgdon in 1954—a classic both then and now by any yardstick. More recently, the design has inspired the building of others like her, even though it clearly placed a premium on aesthetics. *Minaret* is one of perhaps a half dozen additional boats built from design 89, each one very much a classic that sails as well as it looks. And if you doubt that they're fast or that a ketch isn't close-winded, try keeping up with *Minaret*. I have, unsuccessfully.

LOA: 33'0"   Beam: 8'6"
Designed by L. Francis Herreshoff
Built 1981 by Lee's Boat Shop, Rockland, Maine
Photographed at Brooklin, Maine

QUIET TUNE

A ketch-rigged daysailer

Early morning light on a mirrorlike water surface enhances any boat, even one that looks good in all conditions. L. Francis Herreshoff designed *Quiet Tune* for an owner who wanted strictly a daysailer; he wasn't interested in cruising. Both owner and designer were after a rig adaptable to a wide range of winds—thus the ketch. The shallow, self-bailing cockpit favors sprawling rather than sitting, but when you are positioned so close to the water there is a great sensation of speed. Of course, *Quiet Tune* is slippery and as the wind breezes up she really begins to move. Douse the mizzen just when she dips her lee rail and you have the equivalent of a single reef. Other sail combinations are many, but one of the handiest is jib and mizzen with main furled.

LOA: 29'6"   Beam: 7'10"
Designed by L. Francis Herreshoff
Built 1945 by Hodgdon Bros., East Boothbay, Maine
Photographed on the Mystic River, Connecticut, and
    in Coecles Harbor, New York

GRACE

A Center Harbor 31 ketch

The owner of this newly built ketch had long admired L. Francis Herreshoff's lovely *Quiet Tune* design and wanted to retain that same ambiance but include some basic cruising accommodations. With this objective in mind, and a few ideas of his own, *Grace*'s designer drew plans that, although loosely based on *Quiet Tune*, show a slipperier underbody from which hang a spade rudder and a fin keel. Calculations indicated that light-air performance would improve with more sail area, so *Grace* has a rig that's some 26 percent larger than *Quiet Tune*'s. Client, designer, and builder all agreed on a cold-molded hull instead of traditional plank-on-frame construction. Launched in the spring of 1996, *Grace* has proven to be a boat admired as much for her stiffness and speed as she is for her good looks.

LOA: 31'1"   Beam: 8'5"
Designed by Joel White
Built 1996 by Brooklin Boat Yard, Brooklin, Maine
Photographed on Eggemoggin Reach, Maine

STARLIGHT

A Concordia yawl

Starlight is the 23rd boat of the well-known 103-boat class whose basic design dates from 1938. The idea behind the design was to produce a good sea boat that was both beautiful and fun to sail. Although immunity to changing styles wasn't a requisite back then, it's proven an additional virtue: all of the 103 Concordias are still with us.

As this Concordia yawl enjoys an early morning reflection of herself in the still water, let's do a little reflecting ourselves on what's going on. Secure in her cradle, she's been let down the railway, where she awaits the rising tide to swell her bottom planking and tighten any leaky seams. An early spring launching (before drying-out occurs) usually makes this precaution unnecessary, but *Starlight* has undergone repair inside a heated shop, so she's drier than usual. Once fully rigged and afloat, she'll spend at least a week soaking up—her hull gaining strength as it continues to swell—before serious sailing and cruising commences.

LOA: 39'10"   Beam: 10'0"
Designed by Concordia Co., Inc.
Built 1954 by Abeking & Rasmussen, Lemwerder,
    Germany
Photographed in mid-coast Maine

MERMAID AND HARBINGER

On Eggemoggin Reach, Maine

Their spinnakers filled by the afternoon southerly wind, the ketch *Mermaid* and the Concordia yawl *Harbinger* are shown here nearing the finish line neck and neck in the annual Eggemoggin Reach Regatta off Brooklin, Maine. Out of sight ahead and behind were the hundred or so other yachts competing in the race. A few of them also elected to use spinnakers and mizzen staysails, but most were cruising craft fitted only with working sails. Because of the wide array of entries in this regatta, the winner is always determined by handicapping—complex calculations based on the boat's basic hull and sail-area measurements. The resulting time allowances are then applied to each boat's elapsed time over the racecourse. Thus a small, slow boat without a spinnaker has—theoretically at least—a chance to win, even though she may appear hopelessly behind the leaders in crossing the finish line.

At other times these versatile boats become excellent coastal cruisers. Daysailing, too, is an option as the flawlessly maintained *Mermaid* demonstrates as she sets out close hauled on this lovely afternoon.

MERMAID (*Sail No. 446*)
LOA: 45'8"   Beam: 11'6"
Designed by Sparkman & Stephens, Inc.
Built 1957 by Paul E. Luke, East Boothbay, Maine

HARBINGER (*Sail No. 448*)
LOA: 39'10"   Beam: 10'0"
Designed by Concordia Co., Inc.
Built 1957 by Abeking & Rasmussen, Lemwerder,
*   Germany*

FARAWAY

A keel/centerboard yawl

Maine's weather is notoriously fickle, and anyone who tries to extend its brief sailing season risks encountering some real surprises. April launchings may well feature a snow-covered deck and a scene that looks like February. Not a day for sailing, but one suited for enjoying the haunting stillness of a spectacular morning. The dark spruces frosted with new snow are endlessly beautiful in themselves, but with a couple of freshly painted and varnished wooden yachts in the foreground, the sight is unforgettable.

Some of the very best cruising boats are the shallow-bodied ones that can anchor in a couple of feet less water than their full-keeled sisters. With centerboard raised, *Faraway* draws only 4 feet 3 inches. Besides extending the options for cruising, her keel-centerboard configuration and yawl rig became a popular combination for racing during the 1950s and 1960s when the handicapping rules favored this and similar designs.

LOA: 43'0"   Beam: 11'9"
Designed by Sparkman & Stephens, Inc.
Built 1957 by Tøre Holm, Gamleby, Sweden
Photographed in mid-coast Maine

ABIGAIL

A cruising ketch

In the 1950s, boats like *Abigail* benefited greatly from the use of bronze and other nonferrous fastenings instead of Depression-era galvanized iron and steel. Besides having top-quality screws and bolts, *Abigail*'s decks and railcaps are teak, her backbone and frames are white oak, and her hull is double-planked with cedar and mahogany and internally strapped with bronze—creating a more durable structure than the typical cruising boat built only two decades earlier. Realizing the importance of quality construction, *Abigail*'s young and enthusiastic new owners passed over a number of boats on the market before their search ended, happily, with this one. Since *Abigail* will earn part of her keep through chartering, full headroom was another sought-after feature. To achieve it in a boat of this size, the hull must be either deep underwater or high above it. *Abigail* is a compromise, but her generous freeboard has been made handsome by lots of sheer and a contrasting color on bulwark and boottop.

LOA: 39'0"   Beam: 11'0"
Designed by John G. Alden
Built 1956 by Seth Persson, Saybrook, Connecticut
Photographed on Eggemoggin Reach, Maine

MIMI ROSE

A cruising cutter

It's always enlightening to watch experience have an impact on the creation of a new boat. Such was the case with Bill Page, who brought *Mimi Rose* to fruition. Ever since high school, Bill has loved and lived boats: He's run a boatyard, built several boats, and cruised extensively in a variety of Page family craft. During his many years as a yacht broker, examining other people's boats became a way of life for Bill—and he knows what he likes. With considerable input of his own, Bill commissioned a new design from Bob Baker, who managed to draw a most handsome profile before he died in 1983. Joel White took over from there, developing the lines, construction, and sail plans. As with his previous boat, *Sandpiper*, Bill had Gordon Swift build *Mimi Rose*'s hull in New Hampshire, then he trucked it home to Maine. Several years of careful thought and meticulous work later, Bill completed the project himself—a job to be proud of. Her natural-finished interior of clear white pine, black locust, and cherry is especially elegant. Reports from owner-builder Page, designer White, and surveyor Giffy Full indicate that *Mimi Rose* performs as well as she looks.

LOA: 32'0"   Beam: 10'0"
Designed by Robert H. Baker and Joel M. White
Built 1991 by Gordon Swift, Kensington, New
*   Hampshire, and William C. Page, Camden, Maine*
Photographed on Eggemoggin Reach, Maine

INTERNATIONAL ONE-DESIGNS

Racing sloops

During sailing season, a hull's shapeliest part often is hidden beneath the water, so a boat storage shed is a superb spot for appreciating the beautiful reversing curves of a boat's underbody. Here in Ralph Stanley's shed in Southwest Harbor, Maine, we have a couple of half-century-old International One-Design sloops (in near-perfect condition) and, just showing at the right, a Friendship sloop. All are lovely to look at whether afloat or ashore. Even the dinghies in the foreground have shapes worthy of close inspection. Come spring, after a winter under cover and with fresh coats of paint and varnish, these fine traditional craft will be underway again, joining the many other handsome wooden boats that enhance coves and harbors all along the coast of Maine.

LOA: 33'2"   Beam: 6'9"
Designed and built 1937 by Bjarne Aas, Fredrikdstad,
*   Norway*
Photographed at Mount Desert Island, Maine

BUTTERCUP

A *spidsgatter sloop*

It's curious that more of these wonderful little double-enders weren't built, because they have a host of advantages over most other 26-footers. There's full headroom under the cabin trunk; a little diesel fits under the self-bailing cockpit; the below-decks seating and sleeping arrangements are first-class for two persons; stowage space is ample; and, best of all, *Buttercup* and her two sisters are striking in appearance. I have long admired the design, and now, after sailing *Buttercup* for this photo, I can vouch for the performance as well. Of course, these are expensive boats to build, and they have to be extremely well done to look right. High-quality construction was always a priority of designer K. Aage Nielsen, and that—along with his Danish heritage—led him back to Denmark and the A. Walsted yard. Because Nielsen's double-enders so clearly have Danish roots, his choice of builder for *Buttercup* seems especially appropriate.

LOA: 26'0"   Beam: 9'0"
Designed by K. Aage Nielsen
Built 1966 by A. Walsted Baadevaerft, Thurø,
  Denmark
Photographed off Stonington, Connecticut

CLOVER

A Gulf Stream 30 sloop

With *Clover*'s brand-new sails trimmed to the dying breeze, her owners can enjoy not only the spectacular summer sunset but also the speed at which their boat moves through the water. She seems to fly! *Clover* is one of the exquisite Gulf Stream 30s built near the end of the production wooden-boat era. Conceived to sleep four, sail reasonably fast, rate well under the prevailing racing rules, and be very eye-catching, this design is an exceptional blend of the elements that create a good boat no matter what the era. Because they're lightly built and show it in details such as handgrabs, coamings, and hatches, these boats give the impression of being too delicate for strength and longevity. Not so, as *Clover* and her sisters have demonstrated. All they require is the reasonable care that comes from being understood and appreciated.

LOA: 29'7"   Beam: 8'0"
Designed by Sparkman & Stephens, Inc.
Built 1958 by Robert E. Derecktor, Mamaroneck,
    New York
Photographed in mid-coast Maine

CHAPTER II

POWERBOATS

Compared to a sailboat of the same overall length, a powerboat generally has more interior space, weighs less, and can operate in shallower water—distinct advantages to be sure. At sea, weather can revise any scheduled run, but power will usually get you from here to there more predictably and faster than sail. Diesel engines are the most popular powerplants these days. They're simple, reliable, burn non-explosive fuel, and run efficiently. But there are other choices, each with its loyal following. Gasoline engines have more power for their weight and operate with less noise and smell. Electric power, now regaining favor, works nicely in small craft on short runs and operates in near silence. Steam plants also run quietly and have their own kind of charm, as in the steam launch *Walter & Edgar*.

When you watch a steam-powered launch glide silently by, it is easy to understand why so many find delight in this means of propulsion. The focus of the enthusiasts, of course, usually is on the boiler and engine—plus all the piping, valves, and other elements that make the system function—so it's not surprising that the boat itself takes a back seat. In *Walter & Edgar*, however, there's a wonderful marriage between a great powerplant and a great boat. Although privately owned, she has been a welcome addition to Mystic Seaport's waterfront in past years because she fits so well into the museum's historic theme. Visitors are in for a treat when her boiler is fired up and this lovely fantail-sterned launch runs along the shoreline, but even when shut down and at rest, she's a first-class exhibit.

WALTER & EDGAR, *a steam launch* LOA: 30'0"   Beam: 7'0"   *Built about 1895 and restored from derelict 1984 by Gary Weisenburger, Oakdale, Connecticut Photographed on the Mystic River, Connecticut*

COCKTAIL BETTY

A junior runabout

The first gasoline boat engines were heavy for their horsepower, so the small motorboats that used them were slow. In a few short years, however, automotive-type engines having more power for the same weight became available. The boats in which they were installed—fitted with touring-car seating, steering, and engine controls—became known as runabouts or autoboats rather than launches. As standardized offerings and production-line building techniques brought prices ever downward, more powerful engines and planing-type hulls allowed ever higher speeds. The evolution became a revolution against the previous year's models, and during the buying frenzy of the 1920s when speedboats became the rage, boatbuilding companies that didn't keep up with the times didn't survive. One 1929 casualty was the Fay & Bowen Engine Company, which had continued to produce conservative, practical, superbly built, but slower out-of-style runabouts like *Cocktail Betty*. In the long run, however, excellence is what counts, not contemporary popularity. So measured, Fay & Bowen boats stand tall.

LOA: 24'0"   Beam: 5'0"
*Designed and built 1926 by the Fay & Bowen Engine
   Co., Geneva, New York*
Photographed on Lake Placid, New York

GRAMP

A V-bottomed launch

For most sailors, the name William H. Hand, Jr., brings to mind motorsailers and rugged schooner yachts, but it was with V-bottomed launches like *Gramp* that he started his career. In the years before World War I, when inboard engines for boats first became available, Hand turned out design after design of these speedy and easy-to-build craft, which became widely known as "Hand V-bottoms." Hundreds were built, many by amateurs, but few besides *Gramp* have survived. Her early engine has been shed for a 6-cylinder Chevrolet, and with that wide open, *Gramp* splits the waves like a knife going through soft butter. You may get wet, but you'll get where you're going quickly and safely—just the way Hand planned it.

LOA: 25′0″   Beam: 5′10″
Designed by William H. Hand, Jr.
Built 1915 by L. West and George P.P. Bonnell,
    Port Chester, New York
Photographed on Penobscot Bay, Maine

HARMONY

A Pulsifer Hampton

At the rate of four a year, and working mostly alone, Dick Pulsifer had completed 79 Hampton boats by the summer of 2000. With that kind of experience, you can count on a durable and reliable craft, and that's just what keeps new customers coming. Inevitably, these owners become loyal friends of the builder and, often as not, of each other. The engine lives in a small sound-dampened box, so that making space for a crowd of passengers is simply a matter of striking the canvas spray hood. Hampton boats have always been planked with long strips of clear white pine nailed to each other and to the wide-spaced frames. With careful, wood-to-wood fits, no caulking or bedding or glue is required, yet the hulls have proven watertight. For those who can live with a 10-knot top speed, enjoy unlimited visibility, and like to camp out, these simple launches provide lots of enjoyment, running all the while on no more than a half-gallon of diesel fuel per hour.

LOA: 22'0"   Beam: 6'8"
Modeled by Charles Gomes
Built 1992 by Richard S. Pulsifer, Brunswick, Maine
Photographed off Mt. Desert Island, Maine

MEADOWS

A Down East launch

Driving an open launch idling past a shoreline of hardwoods is an ideal way of enjoying the fall foliage. High tide lets you run so close along the granite ledges that you can almost touch the leaves. Here you navigate at least partly by eye, watching for boulders and shallow spots through the still, transparent water. New England boat owners make these bright autumn days count, realizing that in a week or two pleasure boating will end and the shoreline color will disappear. Launches serve other needs, usually in fair summer weather and often with their cockpits filled with passengers. *Meadows'* hull is modeled along the lines of a 1950s-vintage Maine lobsterboat, but she was finished fancier with teak deck and varnished transom and trim.

LOA: 30'3"   Beam: 8'0"
Built 1955 by Arno Day, Brooklin, Maine
Photographed off Deer Isle, Maine

EDNA KATHLEEN

A Maine picnic boat

If this were an Eskimo kayak or a model airplane, you'd be looking at the permanent skeleton ready for a covering of skin or tissue paper. As it is, the next step will be bending steam-softened oak frames *inside* the framework you see here, and clamping each frame tightly against the longitudinal stringers (known to boatbuilders as ribbands) until it cools. Planking follows the framing, starting from the bottom, with the ribbands being removed as the planks take their place. After planking, the shape-giving molds around which the ribbands are bent will be taken out so the boat's interior can be completed. Then, of what shows here, only the boat's painted backbone will remain.

West Coast builders go at this process differently, in that they bend the frames *outside* more widely-spaced stringers, and some of those stringers become permanent parts of the boat. Both techniques produce equally good boats come launching day, but each builder prefers to stick with his own tradition, demonstrating that there's more than one way to get fine results.

LOA: 28'0"   Beam: 8'6"
Designed by Arno Day
Built 1994 by Frank L. Day, Jr., Brooklin, Maine

CHARLENA

A converted lobsterboat

Charlena has proven to be remarkably adaptable during her nearly sixty years, and she's ideal in her current role as the pleasure boat servicing this island camp in Maine (facing page). For the first half of her life, *Mary*—as she was then named— served her builder as his lobsterboat, wearing out a couple of engines in the process. In between, she's been a boatyard workboat and a dive boat for gathering scallops. Not long ago, *Charlena* completed a comfortable cruise from Maine to the Chesapeake, poking along at an economical 6 knots. Throughout her life, few alterations have been made, despite her varied assignments. Perhaps it's because, unlike most Maine lobsterboats, her engine is in the cockpit, allowing for reasonable accommodations for two in the cabin. Or it could be due to her low freeboard—which makes it easy to get aboard from a dinghy, then haul the dinghy into its chocks on the aft deck—as easy, in fact, as lifting a lobster trap over the rail. Who knows, maybe no one chose to make drastic changes in *Charlena* simply because Newell McLain planned her so well and built her to look so good!

LOA: 31'0"   Beam: 8'0"
Modeled and built 1943 by Newell McLain,
  Thomaston, Maine
Photographed in mid-coast Maine

KITTIWAKE II

A power cruiser

Nowadays, the best label for *Kittiwake II* might be "lobster yacht," even though that's a relatively recent term. When they were built three or four decades ago, they were called "Bunker & Ellis boats"—and everyone in the surrounding area knew immediately what that meant. They became the powerboat of choice in the Mount Desert area of Maine, where no shorefront summer estate was considered complete without a Bunker & Ellis boat tied to the float or swinging from its private mooring. Although wooden-hulled Bunker & Ellis boats haven't been built in years, a number of them, as well-maintained as ever, still grace the local scene. *Kittiwake II*, however, under owners Giffy and Charlotte Full, went farther afield. Until 1995, she was their home afloat, and each fall she pointed her bow toward the warmth of Florida, returning each spring to resume cruising the coast of Maine.

LOA: 44'0"   Beam: 13'0"
Designed by Raymond Bunker
Built 1964 by Bunker & Ellis, Manset, Maine
Photographed in mid-coast Maine

FOTO

A photo chase boat

In 1929, Morris Rosenfeld chose his new boat's designer for his special ability with fast, planing hulls. Not surprisingly, F.K. Lord drew a V-bottomed craft and gave it considerable flare—all the way to the transom to keep down the spray. As the leading marine photographer of the era, Rosenfeld knew that a lens coated with even the slightest mist of salt spray wouldn't produce the kind of quality pictures he and his clients demanded. And to chase a racing fleet of sailing yachts and maneuver to set up shot after shot, his new boat had to be substantially faster than its quarry. *Foto*, Rosenfeld's third and last boat carrying that name, served Rosenfeld and his sons for half a century. Before they sold *Foto* in 1977, the Rosenfelds had shot more than a million photographs from her cockpit. *Foto* exists today because of Edmund Cutts of Oxford, Maryland, who rescued and carefully restored her.

LOA: 33'6"   Beam: 8'10"
Designed by F.K. Lord
Built 1929 by Kanno Boat Builders, Inc., City Island,
*   New York*
Photographed at Oxford, Maryland

TYPHOON

A gentleman's runabout

Barrel-backed and double-ended, this scaled-down version of Edsel Ford's original 40-foot *Typhoon* embodies the finest in appropriate authenticity. Outwardly, she's as near to the 1920s original as you are ever likely to see, yet a modern, souped-up V-8 engine lies hidden under her flush hatches. Also inconspicuous are the state-of-the-art adhesives and synthetics that add strength and durablilty to her narrow, V-bottomed hull. This successful blend of new and old calls for a deep and sensitive understanding—one that takes years to achieve. The creator of such a splendid replica must be intimately familiar with the practices and philosophies of the original designer and builder, and, of course, the overall runabout style of the times. Mark Mason, in whose shop this *Typhoon* took shape, first studied the work of designer Crouch and builder Nevins by restoring his own *Baby Bootlegger* more than a decade ago. Mason's subsequent intense study, along with his relentless quest for perfection, has here brought replica building to a new plateau.

LOA: 33'6"   Beam: 6'8"
Based on a George F. Crouch design
Built 1992 by New England Boat & Motor, Inc.,
    Laconia, New Hampshire
Photographed on Lake Winnipesaukee,
    New Hampshire

MARGARET ANN

A triple-cockpit runabout

When a discussion centers on classic runabouts and speedboats, designer John Hacker's name invariably comes up. You think of stylish Hackers as the Auburns, Cords, and Duesenbergs of recreational boating. They shared the same heyday, and with the passage of time have become equally coveted classics. But boats, because they're made of wood rather than metal, are more easily replicated than classic autos. *Margaret Ann*, for example, replicates a Hacker masterpiece of 1929. Although the building of new wooden boats to old designs happens on a relatively small scale, the idea seems to be gaining momentum with rowing and sailing craft as well as with powerboats. Some owners and builders seek exact copies. Others prefer the classic styling, as with *Margaret Ann*, but choose modern equipment and building methods in anticipation of improving reliability and performance, and securing a longer life for the boat.

LOA: 30'0"   Beam: 7'2"
Designed by John L. Hacker
Built 1995 by Hacker Boat Co., Silver Bay, New York
Photographed on the Sassafras River, Maryland

RAGTIME

A commuter from the roaring 20s

Known as *Little Stranger* for the four decades she was under a single family's ownership, *Ragtime's* present name seems to better reflect her heritage. She is one of the many commuters that were built during a bygone era to ensure speedy and pleasant trips to and from Manhattan's financial district. A half-century and more has passed since Wall Street tycoons customarily left their Long Island or Hudson River estates each morning in one of these high-spirited craft, and nowadays "a commuter" has come to mean a person rather than a boat. It's astonishing how many near-sisters *Ragtime* once had—and, of course, rather sad to realize how few remain. Consolidated Shipbuilding Corporation—which produced *Ragtime*—was, perhaps, the premier commuter builder, and with good reason. It was a big yard, capable of responding quickly to new orders; its nearby Harlem River location made "shopping" convenient; the Speedway engines, propellers, and almost all of the required metal fittings were manufactured in-house; and the balance between the company's production-line efficiency and its custom offerings met the demand perfectly.

LOA: 64'0"   Beam: 12'6"
Designed and built 1928 by Consolidated Shipbuilding
*   Corp., Morris Heights, New York*
Photographed off Southport Island, Maine

MOHICAN

A commuter restored in Europe

In seagoing limousines like *Mohican*, owners were once driven between their waterfront estates and their downtown offices. Dining and entertaining in the summertime took place in the deckhouse amidships, where generous windows looked out upon the surrounding world. Meals were served from the adjacent galley. Privacy for the owner and guests was assured either by a separate aft cabin that opened onto a sheltered cockpit at the stern or, in *Mohican*'s case, by staterooms forward with access to a second cockpit behind the windshield at the bow, where the ride was least noisy. Either way, crews were quartered in the opposite end of the boat from the owner. *Mohican*'s hull number of 2925 reveals a prolific builder. Consolidated Shipbuilding, at the northern tip of Manhattan, once led all others in producing large, custom power yachts.

LOA: 66'0"   Beam: 12'6"
Designed and built 1929 by Consolidated Shipbuilding
  Corp., Morris Heights, New York
Photographed off Monaco

JESSICA

A commuter with a dedicated captain

A perk once enjoyed by New York businessmen and financiers was ownership of a fast, low, sleek, speedy commuter like *Jessica*. Part of the package was a competent professional skipper. More than 50 years ago, Captain Raymond Thombs took over the care and operation of this lovely craft. His boss was Jeremiah E. Milbank, the first owner, whose initials became the boat's original name. Captain Thombs stuck with *Jem* and Mr. Milbank for some 30 years, then continued on with two more owners and a change in the boat's name. As recently as 1994, he was still at it, having used up more sandpaper, applied more varnish and brass polish, worn out more mops and chamois, hung more fenders over gleaming topsides, and handled more docklines than most of us will ever see.

LOA: 75'6"   Beam: 13'0"
Designed by John H. Wells
Built 1930 by Consolidated Shipbuilding Corp.,
*   Morris Heights, New York*
Photographed off Castine, Maine

PORTOLA

A family motoryacht

*P*ortola has carried the same family on weekend outings to places like Santa Catalina Island for more than 40 years. Aboard, there's a wonderful sense of informality, as well as a love and respect the family has for this treasure they've preserved for so long. There is no paid captain, no steward, cook, or engineer for running *Portola*—those duties are shared by those who have come to know her so well. Realizing what a gem they have, *Portola*'s owners have sought to keep her pristine. When family needs called for an enlargement of the pilot-house, the original designer was engaged to draw the plans. And when the original Winton diesel had to be overhauled, her very first engineer carried out the task. Precious few yachts, especially ones as large as *Portola*, can claim to have been so well maintained that they've never needed a restoration.

LOA: 81'0"   Beam: 19'6"
Designed by D.M. Callis
Built 1929 by Harbor Boat Building, Los Angeles,
  California
Photographed off Catalina Island, California

PRINCIPIA

A Lake Union motoryacht

The concept here was a craft designed for comfortable cruising along the rugged Pacific coastline between Puget Sound and Alaska. Thus, *Principia* is a good deal more substantial than the usual yacht. Her Douglas-fir planking, for example, is nearly three inches thick, and her double-sawn frames, also of fir, average eight inches square. For additional strength under the engine, those frames form a solid mass, with no space at all between them. Durable as well as strong, *Principia* headed east after six decades in West Coast waters. Now she has undergone a full refit involving, among other things, brand-new electrical and plumbing systems, and a bow thruster for greater maneuverability. With new masts, new rails, a new stack, a thorough refinishing, a foredeck companionway of varnished teak, and much, much more, she's shown ready for some private chartering—generally a less strenuous assignment, but those who own and operate *Principia* can rest assured that the strength is still there.

LOA: 96'0"   Beam: 18'6"
Designed by L.E. Geary
Built 1928 by Lake Union Drydock, Seattle,
    Washington
Photographed at Stonington, Maine

CHAPTER III

WORKING BOATS

Working boats come in a wide range of sizes and types, their common heritage is simply that they are the means of someone's livelihood, rather than serving for recreation or pleasure. Fishing boats, tugboats, cargo carriers, and passenger boats once abounded up and down the nation's waterways. Wood was the predominant hull material for small commercial boats and a few fine examples remain in service. Roads and bridges have diminished the need for cargo carriers and ferryboats; working boats now amount to only a small fraction of present day watercraft. On the Maine coast, however, lobstering has never been better, so there are still many wooden lobsterboats earning their keep. There's also a healthy passenger-carrying trade, in which working vessels like the *Lewis R. French* are employed differently than in former times, but still provide their owners a livelihood.

Abraham Lincoln was only six years dead when, in 1871, the *French* slid down the ways—and telephones, record players, light bulbs, Coca-Cola, and marine engines were still in the future. When gasoline engines did become available to the owners of coasting schooners like the *French*, their response was to fit themselves out with powered yawlboats that usually hung on davits but could be lowered to nuzzle under the stern and push. Some schooner owners also went for a horizontal make-and-break "one-lunger" engine on deck near the base of the schooner's foremast for hoisting the sails and the anchor. The *French* is one of only a handful of survivors. Shorn of her rig and fitted with an inboard engine, she at one time became a full-powered freight boat. Later, at age 101, she underwent restoration and rebuilding, subsequently becoming a National Historic Landmark. Now she carries people instead of freight, cruising the Maine coast out of Camden each summer and anchoring nights in peaceful and scenic places like this.

LEWIS R. FRENCH, *a 130-year-old coasting schooner* *LOA: 64'6"*
Beam: 19'0" *Modeled and built 1871 by the French Bros., Christmas Cove, Maine*
Photographed on Eggemoggin Reach, Maine

NATHANIEL BOWDITCH

A converted schooner yacht

Although launched as a yacht named *Ladona*, this schooner spent a good many years dragging for fish commercially under the name *Jane Dore*. For this, her rig was cut way down, a pilothouse built on the after deck with a winch just ahead of it, and a big diesel was installed as her primary means of propulsion. She became, in essence, an Eastern-rigged dragger like *Roann* (pages 116-117). Such conversions, while resulting in a less-than-ideal vessel, were more cost-effective than new construction, and weren't at all uncommon during the 1930s, '40s, and '50s. But because yachts are more delicate than purpose-built draggers, not all of them could stand the extra strain. They built this schooner rugged, however, and she came through the experience sufficiently intact to merit a rebuild and carry sail once again. Cruising the Maine coast with paying passengers still labels her as a commercial vessel, but a far grander one as she glides by under full sail.

LOA: 82'0"   Beam: 21'0"
Designed by William H. Hand, Jr.
Built 1922 by Hodgdon Bros., East Boothbay, Maine
Photographed on Eggemoggin Reach, Maine

ROSEWAY

A converted Boston pilot boat

Built as a yacht to chase swordfish and modeled along the lines of the last great Gloucester fishing schooners, *Roseway* has been engaged for most of her life at pursuits other than fishing. From 1941 until the early 1970s she carried Boston Harbor pilots to and from incoming and outbound ships. That duty called for an engine—in fact she has two GM diesels connected to a single shaft—and a cut-down rig on which steadying sails could be set to dampen her roll while on station. *Roseway*'s duty for the past 25 years has been passenger cruises, for which her full sailing rig, shown here, was restored. She's always had the best of care, and that, along with having been so well built to begin with, has enabled her to sail well beyond her present home waters of Camden, Maine, to spend winters carrying passengers in the Virgin Islands. But no matter where she operates, her dark red sails make her easy to recognize.

LOA: 112'0"   Beam: 25'0"
Designed by John James
Built 1925 by J.F. James & Son, Essex, Massachusetts
Photographed on Penobscot Bay, Maine

HERITAGE

A Maine cruise schooner

Maine's mid-coast region is blessed with a sizable fleet of traditionally built, passenger-carrying, wooden schooners like *Heritage*. Except on weekends, when most of them tie up between cruises, it would be hard to spend a day roaming Penobscot Bay and not see at least one of these schooners enhancing the already beautiful scenery. Close up, with sails full of wind and the sun hitting them just right, it's a visual feast. Although *Heritage*'s sailcloth is synthetic, it's manufactured to look and feel like natural cotton, eventually acquiring a wonderful variety of shades and tones. Unlike the stark, uniform whiteness of most yacht sails, the warm patina here comes from frequent but careful use. In today's age of homogeneity, a sight like this awakens in all of us some primordial appreciation for classic beauty.

LOA: 94′0″   Beam: 24′0″
Designed by Douglas K. Lee
Built 1983 by North End Shipyard, Rockland, Maine
Photographed on Eggemoggin Reach, Maine

PRIDE OF BALTIMORE II

A Baltimore clipper

Fast and agile Baltimore clippers became an unexpected solution during the War of 1812, when they were conscripted to harass British shipping. Today, this recently built clipper, *Pride of Baltimore II*, provides an unsurpassed means of promoting the State of Maryland and the Port of Baltimore. Her raking masts, square topsail, colorful flags, and sleek appearance attract attention wherever she goes. Closer observation leads to respect for the impeccable way she's maintained and the skillful way she's handled. Being an effective roving ambassador means that the *Pride* must always be on the move, sailing to one port after another, and showing up for local events or playing host to a variety of businessmen and politicians. Already this active schooner has docked at major seaports in North America, Europe, and the Far East.

LOA: 96'10"   Beam: 26'0"
Designed by Thomas C. Gillmer
Built 1988 by Captain Peter Boudreau, Baltimore,
   Maryland
Photographed in mid-coast Maine

CALIFORNIAN

A topsail schooner

Shown here lowering sails as the sun sets on the vast Pacific horizon, the schooner *Californian* returns from one of the 300 days she spends at sea each year. The state's official tall ship, this vessel logs some 15,000 miles annually, ranging at times from Mexico to Canada to Hawaii, fulfilling the program of marine-related education for which she was built. Waterfront events and celebrations, however, also benefit from *Californian's* presence, and she has attended more than 300 of them. She normally carries a crew of eight, but offshore work calls for round-the-clock watch-standing, so the complement then goes up to twelve. Owned by the Nautical Heritage Museum, the *Californian* operates from Dana Point, a fine harbor halfway between San Diego and Los Angeles. Her design comes from the United States Revenue Service cutters that patrolled the coast back in Gold Rush days, and, like her forebears, *Californian* is sleek and fast and always a lovely sight.

LOA: 92'6"   *Beam: 25'0"*
Designed by Melbourne Smith, based on the revenue cutter C.W. Lawrence
Built 1984 by Nautical Heritage Museum, San Diego, California
Photographed along the coast of California

SPIKE AFRICA

A coasting schooner

As an admirer of the coasting schooners that predated highways and transported all kinds of goods to coastal communities, Bob Sloan set out to have one of his own and to put her to work earning her keep. The result was this beautiful schooner that he designed and built himself, a vessel that quickly became a familiar sight all up and down the West Coast. Even before his death, Bob and his wife Monika had clearly demonstrated that working sail was viable—at least for a vessel as functional, salty, and photogenic as this—provided the endeavor was well managed. *Spike*, as this schooner is labeled by those who know her best, has carried gear for yachts all over the Pacific, towed strings of ocean racers back from distant destinations, starred in films, posed for ad-agency photographers, and given paying passengers some memorable sails.

LOA: 61'4"   Beam: 15'7"
*Designed and built 1977 by Robert Sloan, Costa
   Mesa, California*
Photographed off Newport Beach, California

VELA

A passenger-carrying sloop

Seeking a change from the complications of the big, two-masted, passenger schooners he'd grown up with, and wishing to prove new construction affordable, Havilah Hawkins, Jr. designed and helped build this simple gaff sloop. Then he put her right to work carrying passengers, but only six at a time and only for two-hour day sails. Because there's no need for crew beyond the Hawkinses, *Vela* became the family's summertime home as well. On an evening such as this—with a clear sky, a zephyr of a breeze, and a full moon—*Vela* can be quickly and easily gotten underway to participate in the magic as well as add to it. She's lightly built with outside ballast in good measure and enough sail area to scoot right along when the wind is light. *Vela* performs like a yacht, but with her workboat construction and plain finish, she comes without the high building and maintenance costs.

LOA: 52'0"   Beam: 14'0"
Designed by Havilah S. Hawkins, Jr.
Built 1996 by Wooden Boat Co., Rockport, Maine
Photographed off Camden, Maine

UNITY B

A Bahamian well smack

If ever there was a man at one with his boat and the sea, it was Alfred Bain, shown below at the helm and on the facing page at the windward rigging of his Bahamian sloop *Unity B*, which he built himself in 1950, fishing her regularly until his death in 1992. Setting out from his home at Lisbon Creek at the start of a three- or four-week trip, he'd sail south some 30 miles to Grassy Creek Cay near the lower tip of the Andros Island chain. There on the fishing grounds, far from shore, *Unity B* would lie anchored until Alfred and his three-man crew, working from a couple of small boats they'd towed behind, had hooked up the 3,000 or so conch that justified the 80-mile trip to the Nassau market. In Nassau, *Unity B* would stand out as the most beautiful native working craft in sight as she nestled among the other boats, power and sail, and Alfred joined in and sold his catch, fresh from the sea, to passersby.

LOA: 34'0"   Beam: 12'0"
Modeled and built 1950 by Alfred Bain, Lisbon Creek,
*   Mangrove Cay, Andros, Bahamas*
Photographed off South Andros, Bahamas

MORNING STAR

A Galway hooker

If you lived in western Ireland a century ago and wanted something moved from one village on Galway Bay to another, you looked to the sea and summoned one of the locally built gaff sloops known as hookers. The task might well have fallen to *Morning Star*, since she's one of the larger hookers and was very much in use at the time. With puffed-out bows and topsides that bulge along the waterline, hookers are easy to identify. Most other boats have their greatest beam at the deck or show no more than a trace of so-called tumblehome, but not these. Various reasons have been put forward as to just why hookers evolved as they did, but no one is sure. Beyond their unique hull shape, however, they clearly share one important virtue with the working watercraft of every other nineteenth-century coastal community: They are ingeniously simple—a perfect example of form following function, with a lovely-to-look-at result.

LOA: 39′6″   Beam: 11′6″
Modeled and built 1884 by Patrick Brannelly,
  Kinvara, Ireland
Photographed at Douarnenez, France

BROKOA

A Basque fishing boat

Taking in sail was not usually this peaceful for the fishermen of the Basque region of coastal France. That rocky coast faces west and is pounded almost constantly by waves born far out in the Atlantic. Boats had to be rugged and so did the men—and brave as well. Double-enders were common in service like this because they kept a steadier course in a following sea. Oars came out after the sails came down, allowing a more controlled landing, but it's the sails that got the boats to where the fish were, and gave them the power to tow the heavy, baited hooks that lured in the tuna. Outriggers, one projecting from each side of the boat like a long fishing rod, kept the half dozen or so fishing lines spread so they wouldn't tangle. Fishing under sail is now history for the Basques as it is for most other Western cultures, but the building of replica craft like *Brokoa* keeps memories alive, and some of the traditional skills as well.

LOA: 44'9"   Beam: 10'2"
Built 1991 by Itsas Begia, Socoa, France
Photographed off Douarnenez, France

CANCALAISE

A bisquine replica

Amid more than 2,000 sailing craft on hand for a two-week festival in western France to celebrate traditional European watercraft, the three-masted bisquines always stood out, no matter how far in the background they were. *Cancalaise* and her white-painted near-sister, *Granvillaise*, became easy visual targets because of their variously-raked masts; the perky, asymmetrical lugsails (often with topsails and topgallants); the long and nearly-level bowsprit and boomkin; and the high, plumb bow and strongly sheered hull with its low, raking stern. As handsome as they are overcanvased, both of these replica bisquines were photographers' favorites during the festival, and opportunities were rare to obtain clear shots like these. *Cancalaise* was launched in 1987 from the Breton village of Cancale, and *Granvillaise* went down the ways three years later from the neighboring province of Normandy. The two vessels are based on similar swift-sailing craft—once several hundred strong but alas now extinct—that fished the waters off the French coast until the outbreak of World War I.

LOA: 58'6"   Beam: 15'9"
Built 1987, Cancale, France
Photographed off Douarnenez, France

GRETA AND NORTHDOWN

Spritsail-rigged Thames barges

Spritsail barges once could be counted by the thousands as they serviced 19th-century London. Because they floated in shallow water and had easily lowered masts, these barges could coast under bridges on their own momentum. Cargoes could be loaded and unloaded virtually anywhere along the banks of the Thames River. These flat-water craft, with graceful bows and sterns, picturesque, giant rigs, and boxlike midbodies with leeboards, required skillful handling in the strong currents and crowded waterways where they operated. Remarkably, in most instances this special kind of seamanship was superbly executed by only the skipper and a single crewman. Present cargoes for the few remaining barges are human instead of hay, bricks, mud, or cabbages. Surviving barges today serve as corporate flagships, cruise vessels for hire, or as private yachts. Quite appropriately, *Northdown* has been acquired by a museum.

GRETA
LOA: 80'0"   Beam: 18'7"
Built 1892 by Stone Bros., Brightlingsea, England

NORTHDOWN
LOA: 90'0"   Beam: 22'0"
Built 1924 by Anderson, Rigden & Perkins,
  Whitstable, England

CENTAUR (above right)
LOA: 85'7"   Beam: 19'6"
Built 1895 by Cann Bros., Harwich, England

Photographed in the Malden mud and off Harwich,
  England

ENDEAVOUR

A ship-rigged bark

The original *Endeavour*, commanded by Lt. James Cook, set sail to the unexplored Southern Hemisphere from Plymouth, England, in the summer of 1768. In the three years following, *Endeavour*'s 94 officers, crew, and naturalists circumnavigated New Zealand, collected and catalogued 30,000 species of plant life, and began charting eastern Australian waters including the Great Barrier Reef. For Australia, *Endeavour* is as significant a vessel as the *Mayflower* is to America. The new *Endeavour*'s building took nearly six years, three different sponsorships, and some $16 million. Her operation is now largely funded by what she earns carrying passengers and through visitor ticket sales while in port. Here, *Endeavour* sails near Maine's Kennebec River for a stop at Bath, about halfway through a four-year, 'round-the-world cruise that began in 1996. Education is fundamental to both *Endeavours*; while the original is linked to discovery, the second teaches history and seamanship—most engagingly.

LOA: 109'3"   Beam: 29'2"
Built 1993 by HM Bark Endeavour Foundation,
*   Pty. Ltd., Fremantle, Western Australia*
Photographed off Seguin Island, Maine

ROANN

An Eastern-rigged dragger

Diesel-powered draggers like *Roann* catch fish by slowly towing a net over the sea floor. The entering fish get shoved to the narrow "cod end" of the net, and, when the tension on the towing cables indicates there are enough fish, *Roann*'s double-drum winch hauls in the net, which is then hoisted by stages, as is happening here, until the cod end is reached and swung aboard. The purse line is then let go, and the fish spill out on deck. *Roann*'s crew will promptly reset the fishing gear, and as it is payed out *Roann* will do a slow turn to starboard to avoid snaring her propeller. Once she's back towing the new "set," her crew sorts and stows the catch in the fish hold below deck. *Roann*'s style of over-the-side fishing reached its zenith in the 1940s; now, the fishing is nearly all done in larger stern trawlers of steel. *Roann*, probably the finest surviving example of her vanishing breed, is now a cherished treasure of Mystic Seaport.

LOA: 60'0"   Beam: 16'9"
Designed by Albert E. Condon
Built 1947 by Newbert & Wallace, Thomaston,
  Maine
Photographed off Martha's Vineyard, Massachusetts

JACOB PIKE

A sardine carrier

Carrying the fish caught by another boat—called a seiner—is the *Jacob Pike*'s everyday work. As darkness descends and the schools of herring rise to the surface, a seiner will encircle them with a fine-mesh net, then haul back to concentrate the fish and prevent their escape. The carrier comes alongside at this point, lowers its suction hose into the squirming school, engages its big centrifugal pump, sucks out the fish, and fills its hold with them. After she's loaded, it's off to the factory, where the herring are pumped out, cleaned, cooked, and otherwise transformed into canned sardines. Sardine carriers like the *Jacob Pike* support seiners all up and down the Maine and New Brunswick coastlines, but their numbers are diminishing, since the new generation of larger seiners load and carry their own catch.

LOA: 83'0"   Beam: 18'6"
Designed by Leroy Wallace
Built 1949 by Newbert & Wallace, Thomaston,
    Maine
Photographed off North Haven, Maine

GRAYLING

A converted sardine carrier

After 75 years of catching and carrying fish, *Grayling* took up yachting. Outwardly, she looks much as she did when new—varnished cypress pilothouse, steadying sails, and all. Below deck, however, a galley, head, and living space now occupy what used to be the fish hold. For light and fresh air, an inconspicuous skylight rides atop the main hatch. The mizzen remains set most of the time, but to clear the afterdeck you need only furl the sail, cast off the sheet, and raise the boom vertically against the mast with the topping lift. Sardine carriers really make wonderful pleasure boats because their slim hulls are easily driven and they float in only about six feet of water. Granted, the pilothouse affords the only above-deck shelter, but in it there is ample space to sit or stand, and even a berth for sleeping. Hats off to Benjamin River Marine, who rebuilt and converted *Grayling*!

LOA: 64'11"   Beam: 12'6"
Designed and built 1915 by Frank L. Rice, East
  Boothbay, Maine
Rebuilt and converted 1995-97 by Benjamin River
  Marine, Brooklin, Maine
Photographed on Eggemoggin Reach, Maine

MISS ROBIN AND TRANQUIL C

Maine lobsterboats

They say that if a person builds a superior boat at a fair price, he never has to advertise. So it was with Harold Gower of Beals Island, Maine, who built *Miss Robin* (facing page) and a great many more besides. Among Maine coastal fishermen, it was understood that if a man ordered a Gower-built craft, he could rest assured he was getting one of the very best. *Miss Robin* is typical, having been ordered by a fisherman who was attracted by the beauty and performance of the so-called Jonesport style and who had come to appreciate Gower's remarkable work.

Currently powered by a 150-horsepower diesel, *Tranquil C* has worn out several previous gasoline engines in her six decades, including a 6-cylinder Plymouth, a Palmer, and a Graymarine. And she's on her third generation of lobstermen as well. Built as a yacht with white oak frames and keel, a teak deck and cockpit platform, and only a windshield and open-sided awning for protection, she underwent a career change within three years of her launching when Kenneth Dow bought her for $800 and fitted her out for lobstering. That's Ken's grandson Forrest at the wheel. It's his boat now.

MISS ROBIN
LOA: 34'0"   Beam: 10'6"
*Modeled and built 1968 by Harold Gower, Beals
    Island, Maine*
Photographed at Stonington, Maine

TRANQUIL C
LOA: 35'0"   Beam: 9'0"
*Modeled and built 1938 by Frank L. Day, Sr., East
    Blue Hill, Maine*
Photographed on Eggemoggin Reach, Maine

ALERT

A harbor tug

There's still plenty of work inside San Francisco's Golden Gate Bridge for a well-run, powerful little harbor tug like *Alert*. You might find her towing a new barge from where it was built to another location for completion as a houseboat, or helping to move a big yacht to a shipyard for dry-docking. *Alert* has more power than her size might imply. She swings a 40-inch diameter, 3-blade propeller on a 4-inch shaft coupled to a 255-hp GM diesel through a 3:1 reduction gear. With this machinery, she often outpulls newer, twin-screw towboats. As a professional tug skipper now semi-retired, *Alert's* owner occasionally puts her to work, yet keeps her traditional. Steering and engine controls, for example, still operate by hand, and all her fenders and mats are of natural fiber rope, fashioned by the owner/skipper himself.

LOA: 32'0"   Beam: 11'6"
Designed and built 1946 by Martinolich Shipyard,
    San Francisco, California
Photographed on San Francisco Bay, California

CHAPTER IV

OPEN BOATS

Small open boats are practical favorites for many people because they can be so easily built, fixed up, stored, and cared for. They represent a much more modest commitment of time, money, and attention than larger craft. Wood is a wonderful material for open boats because their interiors are so visible, and seeing the structure is somehow very satisfying. The symmetry and proportion of frames, knees, and other pieces, while beautiful to behold, also lead to an understanding and appreciation of form and function.

There is much to look at inside this rowboat from Italy's Lake Como, near the Swiss border. This fisherman, with only his own weight to consider, has selected the 'midship rowing station rather than the forward one, and has rigged his oars so they can be let go instantly without slipping away. When not engaged in catching fish, this rowboat can become a stylish livery boat, thanks to its fortuitous arrangement. Because the passenger seat is located forward of the stern and nearer to the widest part of the boat, there is ample room for two to sit side-by-side. Both passengers can relax in comfort, leaning against the elegant backrest that wraps around to become an armrest, port and starboard. Picnic baskets and other gear can be stowed out of the way behind the passenger seat. In most boats of this type, if there even is a backrest, it's all the way aft, where the boat is so narrow that only a single passenger can enjoy it. The layout shown here could be adapted to any open oar-propelled boat, and if the entire assembly can be made removable, so much the better.

LAKE COMO ROWBOAT   *LOA: 14'0"   Beam: 4'6" (approximate dimensions)*

LEGACY

A wood-and-canvas war canoe

In the days before the Model T, middle-class wage earners by the thousands turned to Native American-type, wood-and-canvas canoes built like *Legacy* for recreation. Responding appropriately, Old Town Canoe Co. offered customer satisfaction as well as mail-order convenience through its annual catalogs. Railcar after railcar loaded with canoes wrapped in burlap and straw left the factory headed for individuals and retailers throughout the country. Boston's Charles River, for example, was choked on weekends with hundreds of waterborne pleasure seekers—most of them in Old Towns. Demand didn't diminish until the 1950s and 60s. Fortunately, a limited but passionate interest still exists among owners, builders, and restorers. Mass production and piecework may have vanished, but each new year sees a few more lovely wood-and-canvas canoes upon the water, and fancy paint jobs like *Legacy*'s are not uncommon.

LOA: 25'0"   Beam: 3'8"
Designed and built 1953 by Old Town Canoe Co.,
*   Old Town, Maine*
Photographed in central Connecticut

ELECTRICITY

An electric-powered canoe

What better way to enjoy nature's shoreline scenery than from an open boat that runs silently? Nothing obstructs the view and even the faintest chirp of a bird or rustle of a leaf comes across clearly. Speed is of no consequence whatsoever; you enjoy this kind of boating by creeping along, moving just enough to gradually unfold a new vista. If the weather turns bad, you won't have wandered far enough to make returning an ordeal. The waters of the River Thames, where *Electricity* is used, are benign, making seaworthiness of little concern. Peter Freebody, whose shop restored and repowered this Native American-type mahogany canoe in 1985, was well aware of how appropriate a marriage would be between the canoe and electric power for a new life on this historic English waterway. Peter's shop fronts on the Thames, and he has long been in the business of adaptive—and appropriate— restorations.

LOA: 24'6"   Beam: 4'1"
Modeled and built 1921 by Salters of Oxford, England
Photographed on the River Thames, England

GRAND LAKER

A square-sterned canoe

An idyllic scene, for sure, but it's a long way back to camp. No problem, though. The boats of Grand Lake Stream in northeastern Maine have evolved for just this purpose since they first appeared in the 1920s. They're part Native American-type canoe with flat frames, thin planking, and fabric sheathing; but they're also part outboard boat, built with a transom stern for mounting a small motor. A mere 7½ horsepower will propel these light craft to wherever the fish are biting. Once there, the routine is to shut down, tip up the motor, take up paddle and fishing rod, and thoroughly enjoy the silence. Grand Lakers are somewhat wider and a bit heavier than canoes built strictly for paddling, so they give the fisherman a steadier platform for casting. They'll also hold much more gear and—if the fish are really biting—a much larger catch.

LOA: 20'0"   Beam: 3'6"
Modeled by Kenneth Wheaton
Built 1992 by Kenneth and Chris Wheaton, Grand
  Lake Stream, Maine
Photographed at Grand Lake Stream, Maine

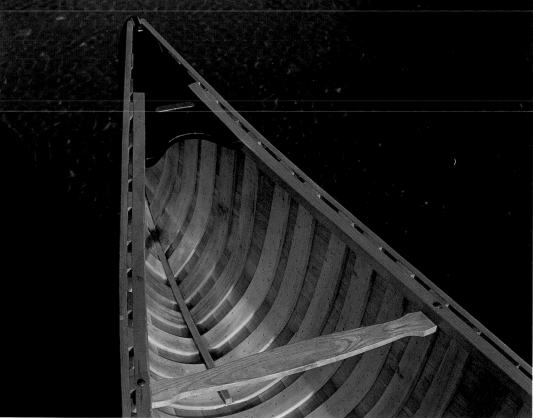

ALICE

A Fiddlehead double-paddle canoe

Built entirely of northern white cedar and local spruce, oak, and ash, this double-paddle canoe looks right at home in any natural environment, from the transparent waters of the Bahamas to a snowy shoreline in Maine. To avoid buying expensive plywood, the builder adopted lapped construction in cedar for the deck as well as the topsides. Both employ relatively narrow planks, so there will be no appreciable shrinking or swelling (or subsequent leaking). At only 40 pounds, *Alice* is light enough to carry to the shore, and, when not in use, finding undercover storage should be no problem because of her small size. For one person, or one person and a child, she's quite a practical boat. Not a craft to venture far from shore, of course, but it's hard to know why one would want to. Skimming silently over the bottom in shallow water, you have the added pleasure of watching what is below you slide by.

LOA: 10'6"   Beam: 2'4"
Designed by Harry Bryan
Built 1992 by Bryan Boatbuilding, St. George, New
    Brunswick, Canada
Photographed at Elbow Cay, Bahamas, and on
    Eggemoggin Reach, Maine

HANNAH

A peapod

One of the great joys of coastal cruising is landing on an uninhabited shore for a picnic or a walk in the woods. Quiet places lie within range of almost all boaters, and you might even discover a remote island like this one (facing page), whose generous owners don't mind occasional, and respectful, use. Another coastal-cruising joy is simply sitting on shore and staring out at the ever-changing scene. Depending on the wind, the water can be a reflecting pool or alive with waves and whitecaps. Shadows among the rocks vary with the sun's location. Mornings and evenings glow with rich, warm light while the noonday sun brings high-intensity contrast. But no matter what you survey—or what the sky, water, wind, and sun are doing—a small, beautifully crafted wooden boat at water's edge improves your view. A peapod like *Hannah*, for instance, becomes the accent—the final touch—by enhancing the natural beauty of the rocky shore around it.

On other occasions peapods serve other purposes, as these youngsters demonstrate.

LOA: 13′6″   Beam: 4′6″
Designed by Captain Havilah S. Hawkins
Built 1981 by James F. Steele, Brooklin, Maine
Photographed in mid-coast Maine

FROASK

A tjotter

In 1967, at the age of twenty-one, Pier Piersma decided to pursue a career of building traditional Dutch watercraft, and he built *Froask*, his first boat. Having served over the years to promote a thriving business, that same boat now is a family heirloom. Rixt Piersma seems to be thoroughly enjoying her trick at *Froask*'s tiller, and, as the years pass, she'll appreciate more and more her father's fine handiwork. Special talent is needed to steam-bend (by means of weights, water, and open flame) the oak planking for round-ended boats like *Froask*—not to mention the fine fits and carved ornamentation. As long as the old-time skills are in everyday use by the likes of Pier, the art of building and restoring fine traditional wooden boats in the Dutch province of Friesland is secure.

Froask (meaning "frog") is a *tjotter*—a little undecked yacht used for daysailing in the relatively calm canals of the Netherlands, where the water is thin and the landscape gentle.

LOA: 16'5"   Beam: 6'0"
Designed and built 1967 by Pier P. Piersma, Heeg,
*   Friesland, Netherlands*
Photographed in Friesland, Netherlands

ABACO DINGHIES

Cat-rigged, Bahamian daysailers

The frames of Bahamian dinghies are sawn to shape from natural crooks like the one in the lower part of the picture on the facing page. Building with "grown" frames is an old method made nearly obsolete by power tools that produce uniform, straight-grained frames for steam-bending. But tradition still prevails in Joe Albury's Man-O-War shop (right), and at nearby Hope Town where Winer Malone builds three or four dinghies a year (left). Bahamian dinghies are constructed right-side up and get their shape from nothing more than a straight, plank-on-edge keel, a stem, transom, three mold frames, and, of course, the builder's mental picture of the finished dinghy. The dinghies built in the Abacos are sometimes partially decked for recreational sailing, unlike their workboat ancestors which were entirely open.

ABACO DINGHY *(left)*
LOA: about 11'0"   Beam: 4'2"
Modeled and built 1995 by Winer Malone, Hope
*   Town, Bahamas*

ABACO DINGHY *(right)*
LOA: about 14'0"   Beam: 5'0"
Modeled and built 1995 by Joseph Albury,
*   Man-O-War Cay, Bahamas*

Windrose and Hesperus

Abaco dinghies

Originally used as workboats, these keelboats have no centerboard, and their hulls tend to be relatively heavy, with a plank-on-edge keel and sawn frames. Their weight and beam allow for more than the customary amount of sail, guaranteeing some exciting sailing when the wind pipes up. Fine craftsmanship clearly shows in Abaco dinghies like this pair produced in Joe Albury's Man-O-War shop. Joe and his brother Jeff are shown here taking advantage of a stiff breeze at the end of their working day.

WINDROSE *(Sail No. 16)*
LOA: 14'6"   Beam: 5'0"
*Modeled and built 1990 by Joseph Albury,
    Man-O-War Cay, Bahamas*

HESPERUS *(Sail No. 14)*
LOA: 14'0"   Beam: 5'0"
*Modeled and built 1989 by Joseph Albury,
    Man-O-War Cay, Bahamas*

Photographed at Man-O-War Cay, Bahamas

MADIGAN

A Great South Bay catboat

I've always admired reverse curves. A kind of symbiosis occurs to create a more-than-twice-as-lovely appearance than what takes place in a simple convex curve or one that's only concave. Just look at the way the light plays on *Madigan*'s stern, casting a shadow and then, as the curve reverses, the shadow disappears as the sunlight strikes the hull again near the boat's centerline. This type of stern has most others beat hands down for good looks. The quarters—the after portion of the hull up near the sheer—roll inward toward the deck while on the deck itself an encircling toerail defines where the hull ends and the deck begins. Just imagine the sight of an entire fleet of these graceful Gil Smith catboats racing on Long Island's Great South Bay a century ago.

LOA: 25'5"   Beam: 8'7"
Designed by Gilbert M. Smith
Built 1996 by The Apprenticeshop, Rockland, Maine
Photographed off Shelter Island, New York

PAMET

An Old Gaffer sloop

This boat's abilities go way beyond what it takes to ghost along on a dying evening breeze—although for this, of course, *Pamet* is perfectly suited. When the waves are big and the sea is rough, this little double-ender—based on time-tested, Danish fishing craft—will bring you through safely due to her balanced ends, her generous beam and freeboard, and a 1,500-pound lead ballast keel, which helps keep her on her feet. In this configuration, the design is known as an Old Gaffer. Initially, however, Murray Peterson designed a motorboat with only enough of a sail plan to dampen the rolling motion in beam seas and to boost her speed a little when the wind favored. As an Old Gaffer (of which several were built), this versatile design became more of a sailboat—sporting a bowsprit, nearly 50 percent more sail, a deeper keel, and a small cuddy cabin, but retaining an inboard engine to bring her home if the wind dies.

LOA: 18'0"   Beam: 6'3"
Designed by Murray G. Peterson
Built 1975 by Malcolm Brewer, Camden, Maine
Photographed on Eggemoggin Reach, Maine

CURLEW

A keel/centerboard cabin daysailer

Anyone who visits Mystic Seaport can't help but admire the cabin daysailer *Alerion*, of which *Curlew* is an exceptionally close copy. Both boats exhibit some of the best craftsmanship you'll ever see. And that—combined with a truly fine design where the hull shape and the proportions of its elements are exquisite—makes these two boats just about perfect. Although in his day N.G. Herreshoff was mostly known for his *America's* Cup defenders and steam-yacht designs, present-day sailors remember him more for his surviving small sailboats, like *Alerion*—virtually timeless designs—and for the replicas now being built. For above all, NGH enjoyed designing and sailing boats like these, and he put enormous thought into their appearance and performance. By duplicating *Alerion* some eight decades later, builder Warren Barker not only reproduced one of the all-time great designs, but he did it so perfectly that you hardly know which boat is which.

LOA: 26'0"   Beam: 7'7"
Designed by N.G. Herreshoff
Built 1994 by Customary Boat, Westport,
    Massachusetts
Photographed off Westport, Massachusetts

TRIPLE THREAT

An Atlantic class sloop

One hundred of these German-built Atlantic class sloops, all for American yachtsmen, left Abeking & Rasmussen's shops in 1928, 1929, and 1930. Most were shipped to Long Island Sound, but several, including *Triple Threat*, got as far as Blue Hill, Maine. Exceptionally fast and maneuverable, the Atlantics gained instant popularity as racing daysailers. Among the first to shed running backstays in favor of a permanent one, the Atlantics have practical as well as truly handsome sail plans. The mainsail can be easily hoisted and furled from the cockpit, and it is large enough so a small, easily handled jib is all that's ever needed for good on-the-wind performance. As the fleet aged, many owners opted for new hulls of fiberglass, but *Triple Threat* underwent a careful rebuilding in wood, replaced piece by piece. It is indeed fortunate that she has been donated to Mystic Seaport, where she serves to represent and honor this great Starling Burgess design.

LOA: 30'6"   Beam: 6'6"
Designed by W. Starling Burgess
Built 1929 by Abeking & Rasmussen, Lemwerder,
    Germany
Photographed on Eggemoggin Reach, Maine

CHAPTER V

SAILING YACHTS

For yachts as large as these, an owner generally hires a professional skipper and maybe a crew as well. Many hands are needed, not only when sailing, but also to keep up with the day-to-day maintenance. With such a setup, owners often have their yachts taken south for the winter so they can enjoy them year-round. The Caribbean is a favorite hangout, and there are a number of annual events that bring together some of the finest classic sailing yachts in existence today. It's sailing season all year where *Branta* homeports, however, and this photo was taken in November. Big sailing yachts are complicated to photograph, and to help set up we usually rely on radio contact. But with *Branta*, there was neither time nor opportunity; only a few seconds were available to us as she passed a non-intrusive background, and we were lucky enough to be there at precisely the right time.

With lee-side visibility cut off by her overlapping headsail, *Branta*'s helmsman depends upon alert bow lookouts to keep him out of trouble on a congested race course, especially when the finish line is in the busy harbor of San Diego. Although built for 'round-the-buoy racing in Long Island Sound, *Branta* and her thirteen nearly identical 10-Meter class sisters were built with decent cruising accommodations right from the start. Because you can stand upright below deck, trunk cabins weren't needed, so the deck has only hatches and skylights rising from it. For six of her seven decades, *Branta* has sailed Southern California waters—but she's not alone. Amazingly, her sister *Sally* (ex-*Twilight*) also berths in San Diego, having migrated west on the heels of World War II.

BRANTA, *a 10-Meter class sloop*   *LOA: 59'0"   Beam: 12'6"   Designed by Burgess, Rigg, and Morgan   Built 1927 by Abeking & Rasmussen, Lemwerder, Germany Photographed off San Diego, California*

WILD HORSES AND WHITE WINGS

W-Class one-design sloops

Don't be misled at first glance into thinking these are one-designs of the 35-foot variety. They're more than twice that length, a realization that dawns only when you note how small the people aboard appear to be; you'd never know it from the design because the proportions are so perfect. Designed to sail fast, look gorgeous, and keep their racing crews well exercised, the W-Class, of which these two are the first built, revives the big, boat-for-boat racing of nearly a century ago when yachts like the New York 50s and 70s competed without time allowance. When racing against each other, the W-Class sloops carry no handicap; getting ahead and staying there determines the winner no matter how long it takes to sail the racecourse.

LOA: 76'8"   Beam: 16'1"
Designed by Joel M. White
Photographed in mid-coast Maine

WILD HORSES
Built 1998 by Brooklin Boat Yard, Brooklin, Maine

WHITE WINGS
Built 1998 by Rockport Marine, Rockport, Maine

COURAGEOUS

A racing/cruising sloop

Arthur Iselin loved the looks of his International One-Design sloop *Hope*, and with good reason— IODs have an exquisite shape (pages 50-51). So when his needs dictated a bigger craft, it was no surprise that he asked for a design with a similar shape and rig. Thus was born *Courageous*, a craft as sweet-sailing as she is good-looking. After five seasons in Larchmont, New York, and another few in Chesapeake waters (where she was known briefly as *Fun*), *Courageous* migrated to the Pacific Northwest.

Heeling sharply in sudden blasts of wind, it's an unusual sailboat that can keep a neutral helm. But, having steered *Courageous*, jammed hard on the wind tack after tack, I'm pleased to report that she remains perfectly balanced even with leeward deck and lifelines underwater. For this and all kinds of other good reasons, she is indeed an unusually fine boat.

LOA: 47'9"   Beam: 10'0"
Designed by Sparkman & Stephens, Inc.
Built 1947 by Henry B. Nevins, Inc., City Island,
*   New York*
Photographed off Vashon Island, Washington

PACIFICA

A racing/cruising yawl

Perfect conditions prevailed for both boat and photographer when this lovely yawl posed for our camera. Southern California's wind gods produced a rail-down breeze, there was a wonderful long Pacific swell, and the subject was beautiful beyond belief. *Pacifica* had just won the San Diego Yacht Club's coveted award for best-maintained boat, and her owners, the Frost family, were justifiably proud, since they had done the lion's share of the painting and varnishing. There's no polishing of brass though; the Frosts much prefer the natural, soft-green patina of weathered fittings. Below deck, the array of commemorative plaques on her bulkhead makes one realize that this craft began running up the mileage from the day she was launched as *Eroica* over 50 years ago, and she's been at it ever since. The same long voyaging and good care now continue under *Pacifica's* new owner, Doug Jones. No question about it—there's far more here than just a dockside bauble.

LOA: 48'9"   Beam: 11'0"
Designed by Sparkman & Stephens, Inc.
Built 1947 by Henry B. Nevins, Inc., City Island,
*   New York*
Photographed off San Diego, California

TIOGA

A keel/centerboard yawl

They say an uninterrupted diet of scenes like this leads to boredom, but there are few who wouldn't benefit from a bigger dose than the world now offers. Even for the folks on *Tioga*, however, it's a fleeting moment, gone in the blink of an eye. They, as well as we, benefit from the photographer's ability to record a view and the printer's skill in duplicating it. For those of us who can open this book and soak in this image of *Tioga* wafting eastward through the San Juan Islands with Mount Baker on the horizon, the sun never sets and the breeze never dies.

When this keel/centerboard yawl was new, her stunning performance on the East Coast racing circuit brought not only trophies to owner Brad Noyes but also more commissions to designer K. Aage Nielsen. Nowadays, when she's raced in Puget Sound, *Tioga* remains "the boat to beat," skillfully sailed—and well loved and cared for— by the Schattauer family.

LOA: 50'0"   Beam: 12'7"
Designed by K. Aage Nielsen
Built 1954 by Cantieri Baglietto, Varazze, Italy
Photographed off the San Juan Islands, Washington

ALERT

A racing/cruising ketch

Day after day, in the summer of 1835, Richard Henry Dana searched for another vessel of the same name from atop Point Loma, the hill in the background that marks the sea entrance to San Diego. Although there are vast differences between the earlier ship-rigged *Alert* that was to carry Dana back home to Boston and the ketch-rigged *Alert* shown here, they share the attributes of wide well-scrubbed decks—flush fore and aft, impeccable maintenance, and stylish handling by a contented crew. Crew, you ask? At first glance, you don't spot a single person aboard. That's because she is steered from amidships. Two completely separate state-rooms result from this unusual layout, as well as a sheltered cockpit. This arrangement became a specialty of designer Phil Rhodes, whose boats are always lovely. Dana, were he around today, would be impressed by this *Alert*'s beauty.

LOA: 62'3"   Beam: 14'10"
Designed by Philip L. Rhodes
Built 1949 by W.F. Stone & Son, Alameda,
   California
Photographed off San Diego, California

ELIZABETH MUIR

An Eastward schooner

Manning the helm of your own boat in a rail-down breeze and watching her slip through the water surely ranks as one of life's joyous experiences. So does building such a schooner as this with your own hands. Although eleven years passed before *Elizabeth Muir* saw the water in 1991, her construction in carefully fitted wood and carefully considered details brought great joy to all who participated in this part-time project—owner and friends alike. No production-line boat offers this kind of satisfaction. A good design, however, is important no matter how or of what a boat is built. This design is timeless, as beautiful now as it was when the plans were drawn 70 years ago by Walter McInnis, one of the very best in the business. How he'd love to be aboard on a day like this, sharing the dual joys of creation and sailing.

LOA: 48'0"   Beam: 11'7"
Designed by Eldredge-McInnis
Built 1991 by Lamerdin & Linderman, Bolinas,
  California
Photographed on San Francisco Bay, California

BRIGADOON

A clipper-bowed gaff schooner

Ever wonder how a boat built 75 years ago in Massachusetts could wind up sailing inside the Golden Gate Bridge looking as good as new? Ever want to know why L. Francis Herreshoff started giving his designs clipper bows with trailboards? The 33-year-old Herreshoff was still working for the Boston-based design office of Burgess, Swasey, and Paine when he and Waldo H. Brown (Brown was to be the boat's owner) drew this schooner's plans, using the traditional New England coasting schooner as inspiration but utilizing a boomless overlapping foresail and a single jib. At the close of World War II, sailor/actor Sterling Hayden bought this schooner, changed her name from *Joann* to *Brigadoon*, and sailed her from New England to southern California, where he gave her a much-improved yet traditional schooner rig. After changing hands again, *Brigadoon* migrated to San Francisco Bay, where she wound up with a 1960s-era rock group. Present owners Terry and Patty Klaus rescued the schooner in 1977, and after some time and hard work got her into the kind of Bristol condition apparent here.

LOA: 49'11"   Beam: 13'3"
Designed by L. Francis Herreshoff
Built 1924 by Britt Bros., West Lynn, Massachusetts
Photographed on San Francisco Bay, California

VOYAGER

A round-bowed gaff schooner

When Peter Phillipps bought this Alden schooner in 1962, he could not have found a vessel better suited to the way he's used her—nor one with a more appropriate name. She's shown in Tahitian waters, anchored off the island of Moorea. From here, it's on to New Zealand, Southeast Asia, and the rest of the way around the world. Earlier, *Voyager* had taken Peter and his wife, Jeanette, to such other faraway places as Greece, Italy, Morocco, Madeira, the Azores, the Cape Verdes, Grenada, Venezuela, Panama, and, closer to home, the east coasts of the United States and Canada. From one of her trips to Lunenburg, Nova Scotia, she returned with a "hull transplant"—a brand-new hull fitted out with recycled pieces of the old boat, such as the iron ballast keel and the entire rig. Peter and Jeanette credit *Voyager* with saving their lives many times, while they, in return, keep on safeguarding her life. As Peter describes it, this is a love affair that works.

LOA: 50'0"   Beam: 14'0"
Designed by John G. Alden
Built 1929 by Charles A. Morse & Son, Thomaston,
*   Maine*
Photographed off Moorea, French Polynesia

DAUNTLESS

A staysail schooner

One of the all-time great sights, and one I'll never forget, was that of *Dauntless* approaching her home port of San Diego at sunset, her rail down, under a full press of sail, surfing down the long Pacific swells. We spotted her on the horizon and reached her just in time to run along under her lee at the day's last light. And what a view of *Dauntless* we had as she climbed each wave, rode over the crest, and then sped on towards home. This grand schooner, named for the Connecticut shipyard where she was built, was rescued by California schoonerman Bob Sloan (page 101) some three decades ago as she lay fallow in Florida's Miami River. She would not exist today if Sloan and subsequent West Coast owners had not fallen under her spell and remained undaunted by the commitment required to save her.

LOA: 61'0"   Beam: 13'3"
Designed by John G. Alden
Built 1930 by Dauntless Shipyard, Essex, Connecticut
Photographed off San Diego, California

AYUTHIA

A shallow draft gaff ketch

Because teak lasts such a very long time, it should come as no great surprise that yachts built entirely of this wonderful wood are still with us. "I guess *Ayuthia* will outlast any of us," wrote Maurice Griffiths, who designed her for an owner bent on living aboard and cruising shallow waters. With steel centerboard raised, she draws but 3½ feet, yet offers standing headroom throughout her living spaces. This makes *Ayuthia* ideal for cruising the shoal waters of the Bahamas, as she was on this day. Her first cruising, however, took place on the other side of the world, along the coast of the Malay Peninsula near the Siamese teak plantation where she was built. Subsequent home waters have included those of England, Chesapeake Bay, and New England. She's proven to be a successful cruiser in a variety of locales, demonstrating the adaptability of a well-designed boat.

LOA: 46'0"   Beam: 11'6"
Designed by Maurice Griffiths
Built 1936 by Alfred Harris, Bangkok, Thailand
Photographed off Hope Town, Bahamas

OWL

A gaff cruising ketch

The British favored ketches for cruising during the early 20th century, while on this side of the Atlantic schooners were more often the chosen rig. Comparatively few of either type have survived, and you rarely find a Bristol-kept cruiser nearing the hundred-year mark regardless of rig or country of origin. *Owl* lays claim to even more than her age and gaff ketch rig. She embodies the considerable experience of her creators. The White Bros., who prodigiously produced boats in all types and sizes, built *Owl* at the mouth of the River Ichen near Southampton. Designer Frederick Shepherd specialized in seakindly cruising yachts featuring exceptional accommodations below deck. One of Shepherd's signature features is a companionway placed amidships instead of adjacent to the cockpit. This means climbing up on deck before you can climb down into the cabin, but it also allows a very private master stateroom amidships.

LOA: 55'0"   Beam: 13'0"
Designed by Frederick Shepherd
Built 1909 by White Bros., Southampton, England
Photographed off Antigua, West Indies

ANNE MARIE II
A flush-decked gaff cutter

This elegant cabin belongs to an English-built Edwardian cutter that has found its way to Canada's Vancouver Island, where she is a floating home for her owners. Luckily for the boat and for posterity, those owners appreciate their treasure and have become its responsible stewards as they carefully work through the restoration. *Anne Marie II* is a flush-decker, so daylight enters only through overhead skylights and four small portholes in the hull. The limited lighting, combined with the rich mahogany paneling, makes for a somewhat dark living space, yet it is decidedly soothing. The setting encourages thoughtful conversation—not to mention respectful appreciation for the surrounding style and workmanship.

LOA: 57'0"   Beam: 12'6"
Designed by Enos Harris
Built 1911 by Harris Bros., Rowhedge, Essex,
   England
Photographed off Sidney, British Columbia, Canada

CLIO

A racing/cruising sloop

Even people with a scant knowledge of boats get drawn to a handsome yacht like *Clio*, just as viewers collect around an original Rembrandt portrait. *Clio*'s low freeboard, delicate sheerline, long and graceful bow-and-stern overhangs, varnished mahogany cabin, and bleached teak deck, along with her overall simplicity, attract admirers wherever she sails. The gilded cove stripe that parallels the sheer, terminating forward in a dragon's head, is an unmistakable indication of her pedigree. She's pure Fife, carrying the original, long-boomed, early-Marconi sail plan and with it her speed is nearly matchless in light air. *Clio* is certainly historic and she still carries her original name. You might say she grew into it: In Greek mythology, the goddess Clio's role was muse of history.

LOA: 45'9"   Beam: 9'7"
Designed by William Fife III
Built 1921 by W. Fife & Son, Fairlie, Scotland
Photographed on Penobscot Bay, Maine

ASTOR

A staysail schooner

Pitching and rearing in long Pacific swells comes as no shock to this sturdy, Scottish-built schooner, since she's spent most of her career in that part of the world—first under her original name, *Ada*, when Sydney, Australia, was her her home port, then under her present name in Hawaii, and finally in California's Newport Harbor. Although now carrying a shortened rig with a staysail between the masts instead of a gaff foresail, *Astor* remains strikingly handsome. How is it that the Fifes—who designed *Astor* and many another big schooner, cutter, and ketch—consistently managed to combine seemingly opposing qualities of robustness and delicacy? *Astor* has plenty of freeboard, yet a sweet and subtle sheerline; she has a powerful bow combined with a fine, drawn-out stern. Somehow, the blend works—and makes Fife yachts among the world's most sought-after classics.

LOA: 73'0"   Beam: 15'4"
Designed by W. & R.B. Fife
Built 1924 by W. Fife & Son, Fairlie, Scotland
Photographed off Newport Beach, California

MARIELLA

A racing/cruising yawl

Many classic sailing yachts spend time in the Caribbean, where regular maintenance is vital to their beauty. Fortunately for *Mariella*, her attentive owner understands the necessity for proper care. The brightwork shown here, for example, has to be recoated several times a year with the very best varnish, containing ultraviolet filters to diminish the sun's damaging rays. Good care also means rigging a full-length awning to keep the deck in its shadow; it means keeping out fresh water (from rain or washdowns) and keeping fresh air circulating everywhere below deck to prevent mildew and rot. Good care means cleaning off salt spray after every sail, as well as removing dirt tracked or blown aboard from the dock. Because *Mariella* is berthed in a marina where passers-by can scrutinize her daily, the high standard she sets serves to inspire good maintenance in other yachts.

LOA: 79'0"   Beam: 16'5"
Designed by A. Mylne & Co.
Built 1938 by W. Fife & Son, Fairlie, Scotland
Photographed off Antigua, West Indies

TUIGA AND THENDARA

A 15-Meter sloop and a gaff ketch

Never has there been such a flurry of interest in restoring major sailing yachts as there is now in Europe, and this passion (along with the necessary skill and funding) brings more near-derelicts back to prime condition every year. Where do such yachts come from, and where are they properly restored? *Tuiga*, in the foreground (facing page), was found in Greece and placed in the hands of Fairlie Restorations in the south of England, which specializes in fixing up Fife-built yachts. She emerged almost entirely renewed. *Thendara* was brought from Italy to Southampton Yacht Services, also on the River Hamble. Pedigrees count. The creations of designers such as Fife, Mylne, Watson, Herreshoff, Alden, and Nicholson are preferred. Finding, fixing, operating, and maintaining brings together owners, scholars, artisans and sailors in a symbiotic relationship in which some truly wonderful past masterpieces receive the kind of attention they well deserve.

TUIGA (upper left)
LOA: 74'0"   Beam: 14'0"
Designed by William Fife III
Built 1909 by W. Fife & Son, Fairlie, Scotland

THENDARA (lower left)
LOA: 105'0"   Beam: 20'0"
Designed by Alfred Mylne
Built 1937 by Alexander Stephen & Sons,
   Glasgow, Scotland

Photographed off Monaco and Cannes, France

TICONDEROGA

A clipper-bowed racing/cruising ketch

There are a number of reasons why this clipper-bowed ketch became the widest ranging and best known of L. Francis Herreshoff's many designs. First off, she's stunning to look at and wonderful to sail. She was very much the designer's ideal of what a good boat should be: long on the waterline, ketch-rigged, and supremely beautiful down to the last detail. (More than 50 sheets of drawings describe exactly how LFH wanted her built.) Her various owners have sailed her to Europe (the last rebuilding took place in Southampton), the Panama Canal is a familiar passage, and Pacific waters have been her home from time to time. She's shown here leaping off a wave during a race near the island of Antigua. Being the first to finish and having the best elapsed time over a variety of racecourses have long been her strengths. With started sheets, you can really drive her, and the larger the following sea, the better she seems to like it.

LOA: 72'0"   Beam: 16'0"
Designed by L. Francis Herreshoff
Built 1936 by Quincy Adams Yacht Yard, Quincy,
    Massachusetts
Photographed off Antigua, West Indies

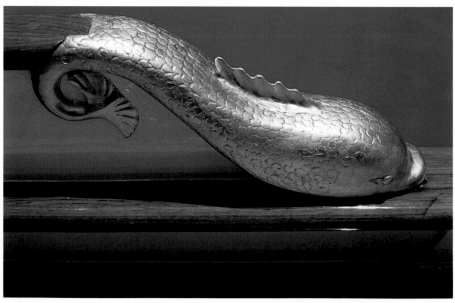

ESCAPADE

A keel/centerboard yawl

The need to utilize the Intracoastal Waterway dictated her relatively shallow draft of under eight feet, and because she doesn't have the deep ballast keel (and the resulting lateral resistance and stability) of most ocean racers her size, *Escapade* was given a centerboard and a bit less lofty rig in order to compensate. She's also wider than most comparable yachts, and the extra beam gives her an unusually robust look when viewed from end-on. So well is she proportioned, however, that no matter what the angle, she is an object of astonishing beauty. It was on the Great Lakes that she proved her racing prowess, winning the key long-distance race—the Port Huron-Mackinac—five times and earning the nickname "Queen of the Lakes." A few years ago, she moved to San Francisco (actually, Sausalito), where she vies with the Golden Gate Bridge for the title of most elegant prewar creation.

LOA: 72'6"   Beam: 17'1"
Designed by Philip L. Rhodes
Built 1938 by Luders Marine Construction Co.,
  Stamford, Connecticut
Photographed on San Francisco Bay, California

189

INDEX